Studies and documents on cultural policies

The serial numbering of titles in this series, the presentation of which has been modified, was
discontinued with the volume *Cultural policy in Italy*

Cultural rights as *human* rights

unesco

First published in 1970 by the
United Nations Educational, Scientific
and Cultural Organization
7 Place de Fontenoy, 75700 Paris
Printed by Imprimerie Beugnet, Paris

Second impression 1973
Third impression 1977

ISBN 92-3-100846-3
French edition: 92-3-200846-7

Printed in France

Preface

The publication of this series 'Studies and Documents on Cultural Policies', has been undertaken as part of the programme adopted by the General Conference of Unesco at its fifteenth session for the study of cultural policies.

In this context, 'cultural policy' is taken to mean a body of operational principles, administrative and budgetary practices and procedures which provide a basis for cultural action by the State. Obviously, there cannot be one cultural policy suited to all countries; each State determines its own cultural policy according to the cultural values, aims and choices it sets for itself.

It has been largely recognized that there is a need for exchange of information and experience between countries as well as for cross-national investigations on specific themes, research into concepts and methods, etc.

The aim of the series, therefore, is to contribute to the dissemination of information by presenting both the findings of such studies and various national surveys illustrating problems, experiments and achievements in individual countries chosen as representative of differing socio-economic systems, regional areas and levels of development.

The present publication results from a meeting on 'Cultural Rights as Human Rights' held at Unesco Headquarters from 8 to 13 July 1968, attended by experts invited by the Director-General to participate in their personal capacity and not as representatives of their respective governments. Observers from certain non-governmental organizations also participated in the discussions (see Appendixes for list of experts and observers).

The discussions took place on the basis of a working paper prepared by the Unesco Secretariat and individual papers prepared by the experts.

The experts were invited to discuss a wide range of subjects: the evolution of the concept of cultural rights in the twenty years since the proclamation in 1948 of the Universal Declaration of Human Rights, factors which affect the recognition of these rights, and measures that may be taken to ensure their implementation.

Unesco takes this opportunity to thank the officers elected by the meeting: the Chairman, Mr. R. Thapar, the Vice-Chairmen, Dr. T. Martelanc and Professor A. N'Daw. Special thanks go to Professor E. Gellner, the Rapporteur.

This volume includes, besides the documents prepared for the meeting, excerpts from the discussions, the reports of the meeting and a Statement on Cultural Rights as Human Rights adopted by the participants.

The views expressed are, of course, theirs and not necessarily those of Unesco.

Contents

Working paper
prepared by the Secretariat

In this paper, a few problems, by no means exhaustive, are posed.

Unesco's Constitution calls upon the Organization to give 'fresh impulse . . . to the spread of culture, assuring the conservation and the protection of the world's inheritance of books, works of art and monuments of history and science . . .'.

The Universal Declaration of Human Rights of 1948 recognizes the 'right to culture' in several places. It is explicitly stated in Articles 22 and 27 that:

'Everyone, as a member of society . . . is entitled to realization, through national effort and international co-operation and in accordance with the organization and resources of each State, to the economic, social and cultural rights indispensable for his dignity and the free development of his personality.' (Art. 22.)

'1. Everyone has the right freely to participate in the cultural life of the community, to enjoy the arts . . .

'2. Everyone has the right to the protection of the moral and material interests resulting from any . . . literary or artistic production of which he is the author.' (Art. 27.)

Article 27 of the Universal Declaration of Human Rights also deals with the right to share in scientific advancement and its benefits. This is an important subject, as indicated by recent discussions of the 'two cultures'. The vastness of the subject of the right to share in scientific advancement suggests that it requires special consideration by itself. It would be pertinent and important, however, to consider science as part of culture in the deliberations on the meaning of cultural rights.

Cultural rights

'Cultural rights' is a relatively new concept. Culture was, in the past, taken for granted. It was frequently discussed within the framework of individual political rights, religious liberty or the freedom of opinion and expression. The preoccupation with political rights was followed up by the recognition of 'economic rights'—the right to work, the right to leisure, the right to social security. It is perhaps understandable that a formulation of the concept of 'cultural rights' should have followed these.

The present interest and concern over 'cultural rights' have many roots, including the increasing industrialization and mechanization of the world. As mankind has acquired more leisure it has come to the realization that, in addition to material things, there is the need for creative activity. A new humanism has emerged. There is a new impetus to match the technological achievements of today's world with cultural achievements.

Moreover, for countries which have recently won independence from colonial rule, this independence has not only meant the political right to self-determination. It has also involved a new sense of dignity, a new searching for ideas handed down from the past, pride in art forms perfected both before and during colonial rule, and the determination to rebuild the traditional cultures so often disparaged in recent centuries, or to protect new indigenous cultures from the onslaught of urbanization and industrialization.

Furthermore, everywhere in the world, as more and more people have access to books, films, radio, television, newspapers and magazines, there is an interest in other cultures and in the rich cultural past that lies beyond present-day man.

Overriding all of this is the fact that 'culture' is no longer considered as the prerogative of the few. There is a growing disinclination to define culture in élitist terms: a new recognition of the diversity of cultural values, artefacts and forms, even within the same country. This may be seen as part of the trend of the twentieth century to define mankind as including all men, each with the right both to create and to participate, to give as well as to receive.

We are confronted with the problem of appropriate definitions of 'rights' and 'culture'. It has been claimed that culture is central to man and that without it no rights are possible since it is the matrix from which all else must spring. Culture is of the essence of being human.

However, the definition of 'cultural rights' is difficult, for it may be said that these 'rights', perhaps more than others, change from situation to situation. They may well, to some extent, depend upon other articles of the Universal Declaration, for example, the 'right to self-determination', the 'right to education', the 'right to inform and to be informed', the 'right to work' and the 'right to just and favourable remuneration ensuring an existence worthy of human dignity'.

A definition of 'culture' may be an impossible task. Nevertheless, there may be some idea of what the scope of the word implies, if only to define more closely what is meant by the right 'freely to participate in the cultural life of the community'. What is, in fact, the cultural life of the community? What does participating in it imply?

Mass culture

Involved in these considerations are the questions of 'mass culture' or the 'popular arts', or 'popular culture'. Varying viewpoints are put forward. It has been claimed, on the one hand, that 'mass culture' is a pathological phenomenon, that it is transient, that it is the result of an inadequate attempt on the part of governments or organizations to educate the taste of sections of the population, that it is due to the alienation inherent in urbanization, or that it is the result of the vulgarization of the arts by mass media.

On the other hand, it has been claimed that not only has 'mass culture' always existed, but that it is a very important part of some contemporary societies. It is further stated that what may be considered 'vulgar' in one age becomes 'acceptable' in another, that taste is a matter of choice and that the influence of mass media—either in the form of 'paper-backs' television or radio—ensures that the 'average' man not only has the chance to create his own art, music and literature but may do so with the knowledge of the standards of the 'élite'. Moreover, the élite is made aware of popular art, and the recognition of this as 'acceptable' proceeds faster than would normally be the case.

Questions to be raised in connexion with 'mass culture' include:

Is 'mass culture' different in value to 'high culture'?

What has been the effect of an expanding literacy on the creation of and participation in culture?

10

What has been the effect of mass-produced books, recordings, radio and television on the right to participation in cultural life?

To what extent may it be said that the mass media cater to the lowest common denominator?

Traditional culture

The preservation of a 'traditional culture' or the reconstruction of an indigenous culture is recognized as being important, particularly in newly independent countries. Coupled with this is the feeling that the cultures of some countries, widely diffused by the mass media, can damage what is unique in the culture of countries which have not the means to produce, in large enough quantities for distribution, the films, the books or the radio programmes which reach most homes. At the same time, there is a belief that cultural interaction is necessary to cultural growth. These seemingly opposing situations have been dealt with in a statement made by a delegate of a Member State to the thirteenth session of the General Conference: 'One of our tasks is that of identifying, protecting and dignifying our cultural heritage, and this cannot be done in isolation from the rest of the world . . . We are evolving a distinct culture and this must be protected from the highly commercialized froms of some metropolitan centres.'

Some issues posed by 'traditional cultures' are:

To what extent are there 'traditional cultures' and how can they be identified?

Does the existence of 'traditional cultures' imply that cultural values, tastes and expressions are static?

Can 'traditional cultures' be preserved and is such preservation desirable?

Do 'cultural rights' include the right to build and to protect indigenous cultures whether they are traditional or whether they are rapidly evolving forms coming into being?

How may this be done, given (a) the limited resources of many countries and (b) the difference in status value still given to some aspects of other 'cultures', e.g. style of life, which affects cultural production, such as fashion or architecture?

Cultural rights and social structure

In the post-1948 general discussion of cultural rights, several issues emerged as a result of viewing culture as something to which everyone has a right, both in so far as one participates in a culture and in so far as one helps to create a culture. Current research suggests that there may be cultural variations or 'subcultures' within the same society and that these may coincide with social stratification. Examples are: 'middle-class cultural values', 'rural culture' and 'the culture of poverty'.

Are subcultures the necessary result of differing socio-economic conditions, the growth of urbanization and of industrialization? Are rural and urban cultural values and activities essentially different? What is the significance of 'cultural rights' in situations where the dominant culture considers that certain values of a 'sub-culture' are dysfunctional or that they retard access to other values or cultural artefacts considered as desirable?

Cultural rights and 'multi-ethnic' group relations

The problems involved in both the preservation of traditional culture and the coexistence of subcultures within the same community are sharpened in multi-ethnic communities where 'ethnicity' or 'race' may or may not coincide with differing culture values and cultural expressions.

What guarantees should be given to minority groups within a country as far as preservation of their cultural life is concerned? Do 'cultural rights' imply the right to group separateness?

How far is the entire culture within a State enriched or disrupted by the maintenance of distinctive cultural streams which coincide with ethnic diversity? Is it possible to have an 'open' society with both overriding cultural goals and cultural diversity?

World culture

Article 1 (3) of the Principles of International Cultural Co-operation states: 'In their rich variety and diversity, and in the reciprocal influences they exert on one another, all cultures form part of the common heritage belonging to all mankind.'

How far is the life of any particular community enriched by communication with other parts of the world? Can we, at present, speak of a world culture to some extent common to all men, regardless of their national origins? If culture implies not only belonging to a particular group or nation but to the totality of mankind, what responsibilities should the world as a whole take as far as historical monuments, works of art, etc. are concerned, both to ensure that they are preserved and to ensure that a knowledge of them reaches as many people as is possible? Does 'world culture' mean conformity with a particular cultural norm? Is there a possibility that as a 'world culture' emerges it will be dominated either by the status value of a particular type of culture or by the greater economic resources of some countries? What is the place for 'diversity of cultures' within the concept of a 'universal culture'? What are the responsibilities of international organizations in fostering the concept of cultures all of which 'form part of the common heritage belonging to all mankind'? Are there responsibilities of international organizations in the sphere of 'diversity' of cultures with a 'universal culture'?

Democratization of culture

Another area of study is opened up by the tendency to democratize culture.

How far is the right freely to participate in the cultural life of a community and enjoy the arts dependent on socio-economic conditions, amount of leisure time available, or education? How far is it influenced by the access to books, records or films in the form of a public library service? What is the part played by access to museums, copyright libraries and special collections and how is access governed by: (a) siting of major museums, (b) hours of admission, (c) prices? To what extent does 'participation' depend on the physical presence of 'community' centres? What is the role of the mass media in the democratization of culture?

Even where certain facilities are free and readily available, the use made of them may vary according to the sections of the community.

To what extent is access related to socio-economic factors?

It has been noted that a significant factor in access, particularly to the performing arts, is the high price that is often charged. This is true not only with regard to the cost of tickets for a given performance, but also in terms of what must be worn, etc. Another factor in public access is the collection of works of art by private individuals. This often removes them from public viewing. On the other hand, some authors feel that the mass distribution of books through libraries cuts sales and thus reduces royalties. The Universal Declaration of Human Rights recognizes both the right of all to participate in the cultural life of the community and enjoy the arts, as well as the right of the author or artist to the moral and material benefits of his works.

Are there situations in which these two rights may be in conflict?

It has been said that the right freely to participate in the cultural life of a community and enjoy the arts is, to some extent, influenced by patrons of arts, art teaching for all children, voluntary associations, amateur groups and the encouragement of art festivals and shows.

How do these groups and activities affect cultural rights?

Social role of artists and writers

The role of writers, artists, musicians, etc., has often been discussed in terms of the fact that in countries where social and political problems are both huge and inescapable, art is concerned not only with the development of new artistic techniques but also with social and political preoccupations. In these situations, new movements in art may be seen as responses to new social or political situations. 'Pure' art, or 'moral neutrality', it is claimed, is almost impossible in situations of sharp social, economic or political conflict, since the artist creates within the limits not simply of an individual concern but of a more or less clearly stated collective concern.

To what extent does creative writing depend upon the right to freedom of opinion and expression? To what extent is the creative artist affected by the participation of all 'in the cultural life of the community' and what are his 'duties to the community in which alone the free and full development of his personality is possible'? (Art. 29 of the Universal Declaration of Human Rights.)

There is a symbiotic relationship between the creative artist and his audience. The writer, for example, is often dependent on opportunities for publication if he is to exist. It may be said, therefore, that a reading public is necessary to his art. Moreover, the public must be literate in the language in which he writes.

How far do the 'economics' of publishing affect both his writing and the language in which he writes? Does the tendency to publish in a few metropolitan countries have any effect on the relationship between the writer and the community? Can writing within the framework of a public, the greater part of which is 'overseas', perform its function as a stimulation to other cultural expressions within the community in which the writer lives? Is it possible for everyone 'freely to participate in the cultural life of the community, to enjoy the arts . . .' where the 'creators' create for an audience *outside* of the community? On the other hand, does a public outside of the community make possible the existence of writers whose views are deemed radical or revolutionary in their own community and who may not find a publisher in their own countries?

Similar questions may be posed regarding other creative artists, including film producers.

In many countries, culture has been closely tied to community activities, religious life and daily living. This is especially evident in architecture, music and painting. The very conception of the individual artist may itself be the product of a very special type of social structure. This communal source of culture may be affected by the emphasis on financial rights, as defined in Article 27 (2) of the Universal Declaration of Human Rights: 'Everyone has the right to the protection of the moral and material interests resulting from any . . ., literary or artistic production of which he is the author.'

To what extent should the concept of cultural rights recognize the differences between communal types of culture and cultures in which the individual artist has a specifically defined role? To what extent do these differences suggest a re-evaluation of the assumptions of the Universal Declaration of Human Rights as they relate to cultural rights?

The artist and society

It has been suggested that art often involves rebellion, or at least that the artist, while summing up the experiences of his community and his age, will frequently be an innovator and a pioneer, both in new methods of thought and in new ways of expression.

13

If this is so, what guarantees should there be to ensure that creativity is not stifled at its beginning? What are the responsibilities of a creative artist to the social order of which he is a part? What are the responsibilities of the community to the writer, the artist, the musician, the actor, etc.?

Participating community and creating community

The participating community may also be a creating community in the sense that a particular art form is a popular community form before it is recognized as a specific type, for example, jazz parties or the steel band, or in the sense that individual creators are more completely moulded by the community involvement than is normally the case, as, for example, the Elizabethan theatre, some forms of circuses, some schools of writing which arise out of slum urban conditions.

Is the creative, as apart from the participating, community the product of particular social environments? Can it be encouraged? Can it be preserved?

Implementation of cultural rights as human rights: the special obligations of Member States

It would be impossible here to survey the various ways in which Member States have implemented cultural rights since 1948. Implementation has been partly the result of new historical situations, e.g. the independence of former colonial territories. In some situations, the recognition of cultural rights has been the offshoot of other factors: education, the comparatively rapid development of methods of communication, greater understanding of the scope of 'culture'. Added to this, in most countries, governments, local and national, have begun to recognize that there is a responsibility to 'culture' that includes both legal and financial guarantees.

What are the responsibilities of national, sub-national and international organizations in ensuring the implementation of cultural rights? What legal measures may be taken to ensure cultural rights and what are the limits of the use of law in the implementation of the 'right to culture'? How do the mass media contribute to the implementation of cultural rights? How, in fact, has education served to implement cultural rights?

Towards a definition of culture

Discussion

A. N'Daw The word 'culture' has been used both in a very wide and in a restricted sense In the widest sense, it really means the very essence of man, it menas that culture is involved in everything that concerns intellectual, ethical, physical, even technical training. In this extremely broad sense, as including the sum total of human activities, culture is precisely that which makes man different from nature. Man differs from the animals in that he has to learn, has not to remain satisfied with his natural instincts, but to train himself, to acquire a certain stock of moral, intellectual and technical qualities which mould him into a cultivated being. In this sense, therefore, the whole field of human activities is essentially related to culture.

Applying to culture its restricted meaning, it stands for what might be termed 'civilization' or, at any rate, that aspect of civilization which ensures that a given people or nation possesses an individual heritage of its own; this can take the form of a way of life, or of a collection of beliefs or concepts; but in any case it has to be that 'something' which differentiates, distinguishes one people from another people, and which it is extremely difficult to pin down or express in words.

We thus have two poles: on the one hand, what distinguishes man as such and, on the other, what distinguishes a people. The latter concept of culture is relatively easy to define, in the sense that it is everything which characterizes a people. It is the right of a community to claim what is native to it, to urge its originality to behave as though it were irreplaceable —all of which makes for its particular enhancement. Viewed in this light, it seems to me that one can form a sufficiently clear notion of what constitutes cultural rights. But when we ascribe to the word 'culture' an extremely wide meaning embracing the totality of man's activities as such, then we obviously come up against a difficulty. We have to account for purely cultural rights. Unless, in dealing with the notion of cultural rights, we are content simply to place the empasis on the ability to enjoy a number of accumulated riches. But, here again, we shall find that other problems are bound up with this. If we regard culture as a collection of values, a collection of artistic treasures, a collection of beliefs which together form a people's heritage or patrimony, this is a static aspect of it. On the other hand, if we regard culture precisely as creative ability, the fact that man is not simply a consumer but has the right to create and to surpass himself, then perhaps we shall be able to define the right to culture as being the right to self-expansion through participation in genuine creative activity; in other words, we shall arrive at a definition of cultural rights which takes into account the potential capacity of each man, his innate ability to create, whether his particular political, social or economic circumstances enable him to do so or not.

R. Thapar   To me, culture has always meant the totality of rights which enable man to rise to his full dimensions. We should discuss an important aspect of the question, which is the extent to which rights are inhibited, eroded or non-existent. Also, it seems to me that as we discuss the details of culture we should view culture in history. We can see the very same culture being transformed from year to year, not by violence or by order, but by invisible forces which play upon the community. To give you a very recent example from my country, our villages are traditionally built in clusters, and, in India, the whole culture pattern is based upon the unchanging village. However, the moment you adopt a scientific approach to agriculture the very base of the culture pattern that has existed in my country for centuries starts changing. As the farmer begins to tend his field in terms of scientific inputs he can no longer live away from it. The field cannot be two miles' distance from his home as he has to live near it in order to be able to watch every phase as the scientific input yields its results. The outcome of this is that over the past two years changes have begun to take place in our advanced agricultural areas, and the first signs are appearing of the disintegration of the collectivity, that is, the village. The impact of this on culture is tremendous. If we go into all the various aspects of life specifically, we shall find that this is happening at every level. I am therefore becoming increasingly aware that we have first to think of cultural rights as the rights which ensure the emergence of man to his full dimensions; then we must decide to what extent we are unable to allow man to rise to his full dimensions. In the complex type of society which is mine, one finds certain people wanting to assert their personalities. That is all, just their personalities. This alone has been denied them for centuries. In other areas we find that people are ashamed of their traditional cultures. They are assuming the culture of science and technology, which is a universal kind of culture. Between these two cultures you get a tremendous polarization. I feel therefore that unless you look at the totality of the picture today—not in terms of what I may feel, or you as individuals may feel about your own individual cultures and what is happening to them—but the totality of the problem, we would be failing in our attempt to reassert cultural rights as human rights.

B. Boutros-Ghali   I shall try to summarize the main ideas that have so far been expressed by my colleagues. I understand that there are some three separate concepts of the meaning of culture. The first concept, of the very broadest scope, envisages culture as a way of life. From this we pass to a second concept, namely, that there are certain cultures of universal significance, of world significance. Finally, we arrive at the third concept of certain forms of culture that are peculiar to certain communities. It is understood that forms of culture that are peculiar to each community co-exist and together form universal culture. There is also a further idea which could help us to define the precise notion of culture and which presents itself under a twofold aspect: that of reception, where the human being is more or less a passive recipient of culture, and that of participation, where the human being is actively contributing to this general culture. Here, then, are a few ideas which should enable us to give a sort of general pseudo-definition of culture. And this leads to another question: is it possible to define cultural rights without knowing exactly what culture is?

It seems to me that we must first begin by defining culture, and then concern ourselves with cultural rights. It would be difficult to define cultural rights without having first agreed on the constituent elements of culture or, at any rate, on a general definition of culture. So I go back to what I have understood from our discussion, to those three concepts which can already provide us with three precise notions of culture: first, as a way of life (an extremely broad concept); secondly, as an expression of universal or world significance (which is already to particularize it) and, thirdly, as a phenomenon proper to each and every community.

F. Debesa   I would like to add something which concerns the negative aspect of the question —I mean negative in the photographic sense. What do we understand by lack of culture? On the Latin American continent, whence I come, the vast majority of the population do not possess any culture. What are they like? What in fact are they? When you get to know them, when you speak with them, you find that their attitude towards life is entirely passive. We have a very apt expression in Spanish for describing them: we refer to them as 'entes', that is, soulless beings, and more especially, beings without will-power. When you ask them what they want, they don't know what it is they want. When you ask them what they think of themselves, they don't know that either. I believe, therefore, that the lack of a sense of dignity and a lack of culture are synonymous. You ask why these people are like this. The reason is that these immense masses of the population have been abandoned by the public authorities, left to fend for themselves for at least three hundred years. They have the feeling that they are of no use to anybody, that they have nothing to contribute to the community. Moreover, they have no community feeling whatever. So they feel useless and without any precise purpose in life. In order to be able to provide these masses of the population with a modicum of culture, it would first be necessary to inculcate in them some sense of human dignity. I think we could add, therefore, to what has already been said here that culture is any human activity which gives man a feeling of dignity.

B. Breytenbach   I disagree with Mr. Debesa, although there is truth in what he says about groups in certain countries having, apparently, no culture left. We have to ask ourselves the very pertinent question: how is it that these people appear to have no culture left? Who, or what, has destroyed whatever culture must have existed (because I do not believe that anyone started off without any culture). Basically, I believe that we are all cultured and this is very essential to our whole discussion here on the right to culture. In my opinion it would be a waste of time to talk about what rights one ought to have if we do not take into consideration what rights people lack at this very moment. This includes considering what has been done to the past of certain peoples by other peoples, and to certain cultures by other cultures, and seeing how we can remedy this lack. I should like to put a few general questions, having listened to what has been said here. We all seem to agree that every man should have the right to culture. I should like to get a little closer to this and define it by asking who is to decide exactly what one is allowed to express and what one is not allowed to express—what one is allowed to do culturally and what one is not allowed to do culturally? What happens in a society where it has been decided that a certain form of culture is for the common good and where we find individuals who, by their contestation of structures within that society, go beyond the boundaries or limitations posed by that society? Are we going to conceive of some international norm which will make it possible for these individuals to be free to contest, or are we going to leave it to each country to decide for itself, and to each culture to decide for itself? We have talked about the right to receive, which I think is a good thing, but this is basically an economic question. When we have enough money to build enough theatres, to build enough schools, to publish enough books, etc., then we can really talk about the right to receive, since it is only really in that sense of receiving that we can talk about it. But what about the right to give? How free can man, can individual artists or an individual cultural unit, be to give? Shall we have to impose some limitations on what it will be healthy to give and on what it will not be healthy to give? This also goes for relationships between groups and between countries on a cultural level. How much can we take, how much will we be allowed to take, and who is going to define what we take? If culture is not static, then which influences can we incorporate into our cultures, and who is going to decide which ones?

G. Lamming   What one has been following really in this discussion is a series of definitions towards a definition. This is very constructive, but I would like to add to the point made about these two extremes, the static and the dynamic, the static being a cultural situation which feeds upon itself, does not expand, is not open; and a dynamic extreme, in which you say the machine is always running away so that one doesn't know what to do. I would suggest that there is a third cultural situation which one might call a liquid situation. I am thinking particularly of the historical circumstances of the Caribbean in which you have the formation of a society which is only about four hundred years' old, starting first of all with the liquidation of indigenous peoples and then populated entirely by immigrants from Europe, Africa and Asia. The whole development, the whole historical evolution of this society is an attempt to work out specifics of identity within the 'liquidity'. One of the biggest problems in the Caribbean has always been to define not so much culture as the identity of each group within this mixed society. Is the ultimate form going to be the realization shaped by what is the dominant official administration, or will it be shaped by one group because of its numerical strength, or a group which has, to some extent, preserved a certain language?

V. Mshvenieradze   I do not think that one can talk about a static culture, nor say that peoples of certain countries are lacking in culture. In my opinion culture is there, and it is always in a state of constant development, even if its development is slow. Preservation and development are, I think, two necessary approaches to any culture. In the last analysis, the very process of urbanization and industrialization is closely connected with modern civilization and with the development of culture—not in its entirety, unfortunately, but the technological, material part of culture. I do not think, therefore, that culture can be given the term 'static'. We must proceed from the fact that culture is in a state of constant change, and, this being the case, it should reflect things as they really are. When I speak about changes, I do not mean simply changes in space. I would say that change *is* development, from a philosophical point of view. I think it is impossible to name any people that is not now in a state of development. This development is very closely connected with the development of culture. If you take culture as something politically dictated, then certainly you are right. But my definition of culture is that culture is the result of the activity of the people. We should ensure that people not only create culture but that they benefit from the achievements of the culture they have created. Culture, generally speaking, is the result of the activity of the masses, and, as such, it should belong to the masses.

R. Thapar   I do not accept the position that it is the people who dictate mass culture, because culture is dictated by political and economic structures.

N. Otieno   I look upon culture as the result of interaction between peoples or individuals. This brings me to a question: can we direct this interaction? If we do so, will we not be denying these people what we shall come to call their individual rights to culture? Personally, I do not think it should be directed.

T. Martelanc   I think we can reach the conclusion that we have to take into account the socio-economic conditions in which a culture has been developed, or is developing; in fact, this has been stated in most of the working papers already. If we start from this point of view then it will be easier to reach some consensus, some shared opinion, even if this is not necessary for the discussion of some other points.

B. Boutros-Ghali   The coexistence of separate cultures is inevitable, and it is precisely this coexistence of the various cultures which can furnish the substructure for a universal culture. I am at a loss how to picture this universal culture, but it seems to me that the international organizations could help to bring it about by serving as contacts between the various cultures.

Going back now to that other idea that all universal culture, as such, is the result of the coexistence of different cultures, I think that as soon as a consumer society takes an interest in preserving traditional culture, such a coexistence is, in fact, produced, and it is by this means that we are able to reach that common denominator which we term universal culture. Consequently, when certain African States express the desire that their culture shall be restored, such a restoration must not be at the expense of foreign culture: on the contrary, the indigenous culture must coexist with the foreign culture. The situation may be compared to the geography of this planet. Just as the world is made up of continents, the whole being included in the universe, so we have a national culture within which are grouped several smaller, sub-national cultures, in such a manner that you find what is called a regional culture, then a national culture, and finally a universal culture which is at the same time in the position of a super culture and the product of coexistence between different cultures. Universal culture, as I see it, is formed by cultural interaction.

R. Thapar   Let us say that we should look at the problem in terms of international culture, national culture and sub-national culture. Could we discuss the problem from these three angles? The first angle is that an international culture is developing as a result of the revolution of science and technology. The second angle is that there is a relevance in national cultures which is permanently under threat (one example of this is when a distinguished writer is forced into using a foreign language and, because of this his very audience changes, and that fact conditions his writing, conditions his editing, conditions his creativity). The third angle is the question of the future of sub-cultures in larger areas. I feel that when you look at the problem of culture in terms of universality, nationality and sub-nationality, you immediately demarcate the responsibilities before international organizations. We meet here, in Unesco, Unesco has a certain responsibility, that responsibility is applicable to the universal sector of culture. I believe that this sector has already developed to the extent of examining the question of urbanization, which is an essential part of man's culture, for if you leave every city to its own devices you may get some good imitation, but most of it is bad. I feel that an organization like Unesco has a very definite responsibility in creating prototypes which are relevant. Unesco has got to move into what I call much more dynamic areas, in order to assist in bridging the gap between the rich and the poor. This cannot be done by just expecting the poor to rise to the level of culture which prevails in the rich nations. We move from political independence to economic independence: but economic independence brings with it a culture stratum which tends to destroy the cultural independence we are trying to attain. This is the reality in the world today. The development of economic independence is a long and arduous process, and the very logic of the revolution of science and technology makes it more and more difficult for the poor nations of this world to catch up with the rich. There is an in-built 'leap' effect within this revolution, and the only way in which you can bridge the gulf is to find certain viable short-cuts. I believe it is the responsibility of international meetings and organizations to find these short-cuts. To repeat my question, I should like to know whether you agree to discussing this question in the three categories? It is my opinion that unless we do so we shall be lost in a kind of nihilism about the future of rich and poor nations. For instance, we spend hours in our own countries discussing this question and despairing, because we already see the possibility that the gap is going to grow much wider and more exclusive. The mere cosmopolitization of culture is taking place before us and is creating precisely those revivalist and authoritarian trends in our states which will lead to many other ramifications. I feel, therefore, that unless we demarcate culture into these three categories we shall not do more than reassert what has already been said in so many documents of international organizations in the past.

A. N'Daw   Culture is the means whereby man is able to attain his true stature. But it is clear that this expression, however valid in itself, does not provide us with a very precise definition of content. If we wish to define the right to culture, we must at least make an effort to decide what we mean by this phrase. Amidst the many values attached to the term, amidst the host of meanings which it covers, its semantic root seems to refer us back essentially to man's creative power. Therefore, if culture is in no way an inheritance, in no way a sum total of knowledge to be transmitted, nor yet a certain address to be acquired, all I can see in the notion of culture is its dynamic aspect—that which causes man to strive to surpass himself. Culture is his ability to create and to understand, it is his creative power; and it is precisely this ability to create and to understand which, for me, constitutes the essence of culture. We can say, therefore—and here I would like to draw a firm distinction between culture and education—that culture is disinterested action directed towards a choice and must be something spontaneous and free.

In everything connected with education, the training of a citizen, of a member of the community, there is a whole body of factors which constitute rights, which correspond to needs, and which are duly defined, furthermore, as educational rights, participation rights and to the exercise of personal initiative. Among all these rights, I think that if we wanted to isolate the phenomenon 'culture', we should place it in the setting of creative activities, that is, the power to act rather than the power to consume. For me, culture is defined by the ability to create culture, and this is not a need but a desire. I believe that culture is at the same time a protest and something permanently present. There is the permanent side to which one needs to refer back, and there is the protest against what, in fact, exists. The very idea of change is a cultural acquisition. I find the idea of change in life itself. Everything changes. Perhaps it is the will to change, the decision to change and the decision to contest which is an acquired cultural idea. However, contestation is not a universal phenomenon, for there are certain cultures which are devoid of this notion of protest. The notion itself is a cultural acquisition of the West, for there are cultures in other parts of the world the essential characteristic of which is acceptance. Despite this, the idea of change is inherent in everything which exists, in everything which has life. In culture there is bound to be an element of movement, a transforming element, an evolutionary process. What we call a non-existent or dead culture simply springs from the fact that at particular moments in time a culture becomes rigid, is dying. In such cases, it is precisely the creative nucleus—the genuine cultural phenomenon—which no longer exists; it has been disturbed or destroyed through contact with a more technologically advanced civilization. Might I suggest that, for the time being, from among the host of meanings that can be ascribed to the term 'culture', we isolate one aspect which appears to be more specifically cultural than others. In this way, I think, we shall be able to reach a more exact definition of cultural rights.

B. Boutros-Ghali   I would just like to call attention to the fact that, in accordance with the preparatory framework of this meeting, it is due to take place within the context of the Universal Rights of Man. We have more or less entered upon a discussion of the philosophical concepts of culture, whereas, after all, according to the preparatory framework, we are bound by certain terms of reference and our duty is to investigate the practical side of the question. How to be able, in the first place, to give expression to cultural rights; how they are to be exercised, and what guarantees there are that these same rights will be able to be exercised. We ought to limit our discussion to the sphere already fixed by the two documents which have been handed to us, namely, Article 22 of the Universal Declaration of Human Rights and the Declaration of the Principles of International Cultural Co-operation.

N. Otieno   If we are going to have to limit ourselves to the preparatory framework of the meeting we might as well just accept what has been handed down from twenty years ago; but we are now in 1968, and I think the time has come to examine some of these tenets. Whether or not we give a philosophical definition to culture, unless we define our variables then even the move to effect these things that have been spoken of in the declaration of 1948 will not lead us very far. In defining culture we can begin to relate the tenets or trends that are common to all human societies in the developed and the developing countries. When Professor N'Daw talks of culture as the capacity to create, or when he talks of it as being the desire to create or the willingness or the desire to challenge existing values, he makes an interesting point. I think this is a fairly fundamental statement which we can examine. Looking at the two societies into which we are divided, I see several things which the two have in common. For instance, I see the desire to challenge the values that have been established in both the developed and the developing societies when you consider the rights of the individual, the cultural rights of the individual. In Africa there is a willingness to challenge existing norms, to try to re-establish the basic tenets on which these societies were based. In developed countries I see youth challenging the present order. Both societies have something in common. Another aspect which seems to be common to both developed and developing societies is the influence exercised by advertising, which I feel is very serious. I think that even the best of us, given this subliminal conditioning of the use of a particular product, finish by becoming influenced subconsciously. Among illiterate people the result is confounding. Values become so confused that the cultural effects are pretty vast. Even the most remote village in Central Africa has a radio. Everybody is willing to sell his goods to these particular people. I feel that we must not underestimate advertisement as a vehicle of cultural change. People, however, are tending to resist it, both in the developed and in the developing countries. They only succumb when they are not aware of what is happening to them in the cultural set-up.

There is another aspect which I think is common to both societies and at which we have not yet looked. Individual cultural rights are affected in cases (which can be found in both developed and developing societies) where several groups exist within a society. The multi-racial society of East Africa could be taken as an example. There you have three major racial groups, from the West, from the East, and from Africa. Within each group you have stratifications which are interacting all the time. I think this should also be considered.

V. Mshvenieradze   I should like to agree with the ideas expressed by Professor N'Daw and Doctor Otieno. In connexion with what they said, I should like to point out that this willingness to challenge culture is the role of the masses, the role of the people, and that this questioning is increasing from day to day. I also see some interesting ideas in what Professor Boutros-Ghali says, i.e. first, that any culture has several dimensions, and, second, that the problem of culture needs a concrete approach. I would say that it is necessary to take into consideration so-called systems of 'culturation'. Any culture of a given society is determined, in the last run, by socio-economic conditions, by the level of production. However, cultures can differ within the framework of a national culture and, in a sense, we can speak of national cultures and international or oecumenical cultures; were we not to do so, it would be difficult to justify the thesis, with which I agree, that the culture of contemporary civilizations is the result of the maturity of older peoples. However, the role of independent cultures should not be exaggerated, as this would lead to some confusion. It could lead to culture being reduced to mere spiritual values, thus creating an illusion, for the problem of cultural interaction cannot be solved on purely theoretical grounds without mention being made of the necessary social, economic and political prerequisites for it.

My last point is that no one common culture exists in the world today. A bitter struggle is waged to retain cultural values and traditions, the rights to cultural benefits sharpening the problem of cultural interaction and so on. However, on a national scale the existence of many cultures leads to a vast cultural interaction, and in this sense cultural interaction is a real process of mutual influence and mutual enrichment. When speaking of changes, I wish to stress that I do not mean mere changes in space but progressive development. And this process is based on the objective law of social progress. Cultural interaction prevents the imposition of one culture on another, the absorption of one culture by another, and it also prevents one nation slowing down the cultural development of another. Who is in a position to respect his own nation's culture? He who respects other nation's cultures. And who is in a position to respect his own cultural rights? He who respects the cultural rights of his fellow men. In this sense I feel that philosophy and philosophical definitions can only help us.

T. Martelanc   We know that in certain societies, for instance where slavery has existed, there have been cultures that we continue to admire even today. However, we also know that while these cultures were being made, hundreds of thousands of people perished; for instance, the building of a cultural monument may have meant the destruction of hundreds of lives. Nevertheless, I am wondering if this is the kind of cultural creation we are striving for today. Personally, I think it is much more what we have been talking about, that is to say, a kind of democratization of culture which really enables the largest possible portion of the human race, or ideally the whole human race, to participate in cultural benefits. This is what I mean by the term 'democratization'. I think there should be no confusion in this respect, no confusion between the high achievements of culture in the past and the aims which we are trying to achieve today, which are to ensure that rights to culture belong to everybody.

F. Jeanson   It seems to me that in the first place we have the problem of the definition of culture and, secondly, the problem of the definition of the precise subject-matter of culture, its goal, its meaning, its utility. What purpose does it serve? I don't know, I should like simply to put this question before we go any further.

Y. Cohen   It seems to me that we are using words which have very different meanings to many of us. One of the things that perplexes me is that we seem to have narrowed down the concept of culture to one very small aspect of culture, namely the arts—music, poetry, etc. Some of us have been talking about the culture of élites, wheareas I think we actually may mean the life-style of élites, that is the daily life-style of élites. I understand culture to include much more than the arts, however broadly defined the arts may be. For example, let me go back a few years. I remember that about ten to fifteen years ago it was all the rage among psychologists, sociologists, and especially social workers, to insist that we must make the masses creative. We must teach every person, get every person, to be creative, whether he wanted to be creative or not, or whether he was capable of being creative or not. I get the feeling now from some of the discussions I have heard here that instead of getting the people to be creative, we are insisting that they enjoy the products of creativity, whether they want to or not, as though this were the be-all and end-all of life. The wherewithall of life is the major problem for millions of people. How do representatives of their groups make themselves heard? It is not a question of whether they can enjoy the life-style of the élite, but of how they can get the élites to hear them. How can they get the élites to pay attention to them or even to be aware that they exist, in spite of the fact that, to a large extent, it is the élites themselves who have created these groups? I think that these are the major problems.

Tradition and modernity

Community or group rights

by Kiyotaka Aoyagi

The definition of culture and its implications

In anthropology, culture is generally defined as a way of life. If one wishes a technical definition, a good example could be drawn from Kluckhohn's work. He writes: 'Culture is a
historically created system of explicit and implicit designs for living, which tends to be shared
by all or specially designated members of a group at a specific point in time'.[1]

The Secretariat working paper discusses the categories of culture as well as the units
of cultures. It pays attention to cultural changes which may be 'desirable' or 'undesirable'.
It also has a few references to the content of culture. Because of this, one cannot judge what
is meant by culture in this working paper. However, in practice, the meaning of culture seems
to be somewhat narrowly treated when it is compared with the anthropological definition.

Anthropologists do not distinguish cultures as being either superior or inferior in quality
or quantity. This basic idea must be borne in mind when we take up the problem of cultural
rights. To distinguish cultures as in no way 'superior' or 'inferior' implies that one culture may
not impose any of its values or its elements upon another culture. There should, therefore,
be no interference between cultures. This should be so even where there may be in a society
a cultural phenomenon to be considered as undesirable from the value standard of another
society.

However, there are a few exceptions to this principle. Head-hunting is not tolerable,
whatever the reason for it; nor is the custom of finger cutting as a token of mourning, as
found among the New Guinea Highlanders. The universal value here is respect for human
life. Eskimoes practise a custom of wife-lending. This is not necessarily unethical or immoral.
It should be interpreted in the context of their hunting life. Culture, then, is very much a
question of how people select their way of living.

1. C. Kluckhohn, 'Cultural Anthropology', in: S. Izumi (ed.), *American Study Seminar*, p. 28, Tokyo
   1954.

Nevertheless, most of us tend to act or react from the point of reference of a 'superior' or 'inferior' culture. Before citing concrete examples of this, I should like to refer to the units of culture.

The unit may include in it family culture, on the one extreme, and world culture, on the other extreme. Many cultural and social anthropologists have chosen relatively small and isolated communities to describe cultures. Undoubtedly, each of such communities is an important unit of a culture or a sub-culture. A community as a cultural unit may also be found in those urban environments where people of various ethnic backgrounds conglomerate. However, above all, the group is the unit for culture. There are indeed countless groups ranging from *Homo sapiens* to cliques in American society, flower arrangement groups or *Haiku* groups in Japanese society.

The relationship between group rights and cultural rights

The most important question to be dealt with in this paper is that of examining the relationship between cultural rights and group rights. The Ainu culture of Hokkaido in Japan is dying out. Why is this so? Not only this culture but also the people of the group itself are near to extinction. Again, there is the Buraku minority in Japan. Roughly three million people are relegated to the inferior status of the Buraku minority. Racially they are in no way different from non-Buraku people. Their culture in its very nature is nothing but Japanese culture. Yet, because of their economic status they have developed a 'culture of poverty'. Their passing into non-Buraku society is as difficult as the passing of American Negroes into white society. It is clear that civil rights contain within them the substance of cultural rights. American Negroes, with few exceptions, identify themselves with Americans, and their culture is American culture; but, how many cultural rights may they be said to possess? Okinawans in general have a cultural inferiority complex, although their culture is closely akin to the mainland culture. Their inferiority complex has been intensified in the years after the Second World War. What would be the way to dissolve the cultural inferiority complex of the Okinawans?

The significance of group rights is prominent in multiracial or ethnic societies. Group rights should presuppose equal cultural status for different ethnic groups.

The relationship between group rights and individual rights

Another problem should be considered: it is the problem of the relationship between group rights and individual rights. The group protects its members, but sometimes it impinges upon the individual right. Japanese villages have been traditionally among the most solid social groups, based on territorial as well as kinship bonds. The group right has been used in some villages as the decisive check against individual deviant behaviour. This is occasionally so even today, and signifies that an infringement of individual rights is made possible by the importance given to the group rights of a community. The Bureau of the Civil Liberties Commission in Tokyo has reported that they accepted 145 complaints of village ostracism over a period of five years, from 1963 to 1967.[1] The group should guarantee that the individual member has freedom to join or withdraw from the group, and this is, I think, a significant premise for the exercise of group rights. Such villages are apt to resist outside influences—new ideas and new modes of life. Certain cultural values of this type of village are sub-cultural values within Japanese cultural values which retard access to other values or cultural artefacts considered desirable.

It is what we might call 'inhabitants' movement' that has begun to play a significant role

1. *Statistics of the Infringement of the Individual Right*, p. 17, Tokyo, Bureau of Civil Liberties Commission, Ministry of Justice, 1967.

in working out the conditions which make it possible to absorb new ideas and innovations. This movement usually starts from a small group both in rural and urban communities. The significance and the right of citizens' voluntary group activities in Japanese cities lie now in the self-protection of living conditions against public nuisance or traffic accidents. It is in the right of living and in the group activities that each of many urban dwellers has been finding his cultural right.

Right and duty

Culture changes. Group members alternate. Groups have ups and downs. Also, the community does not stay as it is. The Secretariat working paper pays attention to cultural change, although it does not employ that term.

There is anxiety over the fact that traditional culture, however unique or favourable it may be, might become dominated by the cultures of larger and more powerful societies. The traditional culture which may give a psychological stability to the people is often compelled to abandon some of its elements in the face of advanced technology and urbanization. Convenience very often exceeds tradition. There is a duty for community people to hand down to posterity cultural elements, tangible or intangible, in danger of disappearing due to competition with modern functional life. To let culture disappear is a resignation of our cultural right.

I am not saying, however, that culture can be, or should be, preserved in its every quality and quantity. The question is what types of preservation would be desirable. Obviously, a museum is one type of preservation, and it may be interpreted as a symbolization of our traditional cultural elements. School education has played its role in preservation, and it may be termed as 'knowledgization' of our vast traditional culture.

As for our neighbours, who come from different cultural or ethic groups, what can we do about them? It was unfortunate that the Japanese Government forced the abrupt policy of assimilation, for instance, upon the Ainu. Does this imply that the government should have done nothing to them, and should the Ainu territory have been preserved as it was? The coexistence of various ethnic groups in one society means coinfluence, and accordingly calls for the creation of the necessary conditions for harmonious living, without impingement, or for integration-oriented living on equal terms.

It is important that an objective appraisal be made of recent experiments of inducing social change or action anthropology by international or other organizations in various parts of the world.

Universal culture and national cultures

by Alassane N'Daw

General

The working paper prepared by the Secretariat covers such vast and diverse questions that any attempt on my part to supply answers to all that it contains would be vain. I shall speak merely from the standpoint of Africa in search of itself, seeking the meanings and implications which the term 'cultural rights' may evoke in the mind of a man sprung from a civilization whose original and specific cultural components have only just been recognized.

While in western societies culture has long been regarded as the preserve of a privileged few, it has also appeared until very recently to be the prerogative of the 'civilized' countries. No value was attached in the West to African forms of cultural expression, whether in literature, in music, in architecture or the plastic arts.

If we are really to understand why certain peoples claimed cultural rights before these were even written into the Universal Declaration of Human Rights proclaimed in Paris on 10 December 1948 by the United Nations General Assembly, the term culture, or at least our conception of it, must be defined.

Definition of culture

Culture comprises all forms of expression, thought and action peculiar to a given community. It includes the beliefs, institutions and techniques which impose the same style of living on the members of a society. It ensures the unity and stability, while undergoing the transformations, of that society—transformations to which moreover it continually contributes. Viewed in this aspect all peoples have original cultures which are worthy of safeguarding. But Africa's cultural claim, the demand to occupy a place in the world as a distinct, individual entity, has always been bound up with the movement for the emancipation of colonial peoples, based on the fundamental principle of the right of peoples to self-determination. This principle presupposes, in the sphere of culture, the right to an original civilization, which has not only to be preserved, but to be developed by free creative activity. This need for creative activity, which impels the peoples of Africa to want to be not only consumers but creators of material and spiritual values, is one of man's most deep-seated needs. For the individual as for the group, after the satisfaction of material needs, creative activity, whether in the form of major works or minor products, is the essential condition of happiness, that is, of the full development of the personality.

Concluding, we would say that *cultural activity* is the materialization of the creative aspirations and capacities latent in all people. The cultural rights of a people mainly involve the power to maintain, revive, develop and make known its own values. The cultural rights of individuals are dependent on economic and social conditions calculated to enable everyone to develop his creative potential to the fullest. This in turn depends on the training of an aesthetic sense and acquisition of the knowledge required to exercise one's right of criticism.

Traditional culture

The extraordinary diversity of forms which man has invented to meet needs that are everywhere identical shows that culture is a permanent human, and therefore universal, fact, but one which assumes particular styles according to the individual's psychology, historical background and environment. Each people has its heritage, a set of values which assume a concrete form in its attitudes to life and in traditional institutions. By analysing a people's basic representation, that is, the images and symbols whereby it expresses man's relationship to the world, to himself and to God, we can bring out that people's cultural background and discover in it a coherent whole, a genuinely established cultural complex.

The static aspect which a given culture may have on analysis, should not blind us to the fact that no culture has any chance of survival unless it is constantly renewed and recreated. As Paul Ricoeur has said, beyond the coherent and closed historical patterns in which particular cultures crystallize, we find a cultural nucleus, which is the creative phenomenon proper. It is precisely this creative power which is imperilled by modernity.

In the developing countries traditional cultures, owing to their fragility and the absence of powerful socio-economic supports, are particularly vulnerable to the erosive action of the technological civilization, which is becoming universal. If the traditional cultures in which succeeding generations in a country found their justification for living were to disappear, the consequences would be very seriously upsetting to the indigenous populations and would entail an irreparable loss for mankind. The protection of these cultures and their elaboration with a view to enabling them to identify themselves with the modern world are exigencies which have their place in the understanding and extension of the concept of 'cultural right'.

World culture and national culture

A universal, world civilization may be said to exist. The essential characteristic of this is the eruption of technology into the remotest corners of the world. It seems impossible to arrest the process by which ways of life and habits of behaviour and appearance are standardized, even down to food and clothing. The development of transport, with the consequent multiplication of human relations, leads to increasing awareness of the interdependence of all national communities and of all social groups. This civilization gives rise to the consumer culture nowadays so much decried and 'contested', but which nevertheless has its positive aspects, in that it offers the masses access to elementary goods and reinforces the campaign against illiteracy.

One method of fighting against the standardization of ways of living and the 'shoddy' values transmitted by mass culture is by preserving authentic cultures. The universe of machines and amenities of civilization, while they lessen men's labour and guarantee a well-being to which only a privileged minority could formerly aspire, do not offer men a *justification for living*, 'words of life' as we say in Africa. The duty to assimilate the techniques by which Nature is dominated (a rule peculiar to European culture, which is essentially Promethean, but to which every natural culture must conform if it wants to survive) is inseparable from the right to make ourselves fully masters of our own cultures. The traditional ways of living must be thought out again and must face the challenges of the modern scientific approach. 'The branch cut elsewhere and then thrust into our soil does not give as much shade as the tree of native growth', says a Baule proverb. Our task is not to imitate an external model, but to enable traditional values to resume their humanist functions, and to reflect upon them to the point where their universal significance is revealed. True universal culture is a move towards man's spiritual unity, but it must not put an end to the plurality of cultures. The relationship of world culture to existing cultures is expressed in complementary terms without which mankind as a whole cannot make any progress.

Proposals for a policy of cultural development

The assertion of 'cultural rights', doubtless necessary in order to sharpen public awareness, is far from satisfying the cultural claims of our countries. It is not enough to assert a principle;

its practical consequences must be accepted. We propose the adoption of a veritable policy of cultural development with a view to making the particular treasures of the community and those in other parts of the world accessible to all. The essential aim of such a policy will be to set up effective agencies for applied cultural research. The international organizations, and Unesco in particular, should increase their aid for the conservation of artistic treasures and the cultural revival of the newly independent countries with a view to pooling resources. Africa, fragmented and broken up into English-, French-, Portuguese- or Arabic-speaking zones, finds in the action taken by Unesco that guarantee of impartiality and that goodwill by means of which it will be possible to rediscover the common basic evidence and the original structures which will serve as major elements in the civilization now being created.

All the latest technical means, including the most recent facilities for audio-visual expression (cinema, photography, tape recording), should be used to solve the cultural development problems of the Third World in particular, and of intercultural activity in general. It will be possible, through institutes of applied cultural research, to restore their authenticity to cultural forms and values which have lost their vitality as a result of destruction by outside influences of the social structures within which they had their birth. These centres will be used for experiments in methods of reviving traditional forms and elaborating new means of expression for inclusion in the new framework for living. An institute of applied cultural research would comprise: (a) a research centre for the arts of audio-visual expression (dancing, theatre, poetry, song, etc.); (b) a research centre for the plastic arts (sculpture, painting, crafts) and (c) a centre for research into cultural values.

In Senegal, my friend Roland Colin and I tried to form a committee for cultural development assembling representatives of the Institut Français d'Afrique Noire, the services of the Ministry of Education, university circles (students and teachers), youth (youth movements and youth clubs), leaders in the basic communities (revival of the country-side). Through the National Commissions Unesco could encourage the setting up of committees formed of research workers, experts and men of culture to draw up programmes of cultural action both at government level and in the cultural circles created by communities, youth clubs in particular. Cultural autonomy being one of the conditions for constructing the nation, the State must assume responsibility for the task of encouraging art and culture without stifling the spontaneity and creativity of the masses. Unesco could assist culture to rise above the national setting and forge the necessary links between cultural movements, and so help to create a universal civilization to be the common heritage of all mankind.

Culture of élite and culture of majorities

by Fernando Debesa

Rather than a generalized speculative view on the subject of the élite and the masses, my personal experience and competence enable me to put forward a concrete opinion on several points.

The present cultural situation in Latin America

General considerations

Deep cultural inequality. While élites have a high cultural level, the majority of the population lives in a shameful state of cultural underdevelopment.

Deep social inequality. Cultural inequality is related to social inequality. The majority of the population live in bad conditions of life, without participating in the advantages of civilization and democracy. Small minorities live in good conditions of life.

This situation demands urgent radical reforms. Otherwise cultural progress can only be theoretical.

Different levels of social inequality. The social situation is not the same in all the Latin American countries. Those countries in which there is a strong middle class (Argentina, Mexico, Chile, Uruguay) have a solid base to lean on, because the middle class appears to the working class as a possible better social condition. On the other hand, countries without a strong middle class have a still bigger problem, because the working class sees only the upper class in front of them, seeming to far ahead to be an example to follow.

Culture and social reform. When improvements in education are obtained, specially through literacy campaigns, social mobility tends to follow.

This is proof that education and culture may become forces of social transformation in Latin America.

Desire for integration and cultural communication. Throughout the entire Latin American continent there has developed over the last few years a desire for close collaboration between its cultural organizations (Ministries of Education, universities, etc). and its intellectuals and artists.

This new approach might prove extremely important in the planning of Latin American cultural development.

Culture and war. Latin American countries have been pitied and ridiculed for their revolutions, considered to be the result of an underdeveloped culture. However, in many of the 'revolutions' of this century, changes of government have taken place with few casualities, whereas in the same period, the highly cultured European countries have twice been torn by devastating world wars, in which millions of human beings have died. Furthermore, it was in cultured Europe that Nazism and its shameful contempt for man was born.

This comparison has the sole aim of showing that Latin America, in spite of its cultural underdevelopment, keeps a sense of respect for the human being.

Culture of the majorities in Latin America

The educational situation is very bad: 60 million illiterates; average school attendance less than four years; secondary education for professions reaches only 33 per cent of school-children.

This situation affects both social and economic progress. In the social field, democracy cannot function. In the economic field, the result is low productivity. There is a vicious circle between social stagnation and low level of productivity.

There are campaigns to combat illiteracy in almost every Latin American country. But the results are not important enough: Why?
1. Because attacking illiteracy without at the same time attacking backward social conditions does not eliminate the root of the evil.
2. Literacy campaigns are not given first priority in national budgets. Some countries spend more on armaments than on such campaigns.

Traditional cultural elements of pre-Colombian, Hispanic and Colonial origin remain in all Latin American countries: native languages, like Quechua, Guarani, Araucano, etc.; folk literature and poetry; spoken tales; music and song, solo or choral; solo and group dancing; children's games; religious cults and festivities; textile arts and ceramics; painting and sculpture; country medicine; the crafts of dyeing.

These cultural elements tend to disappear in the towns and regions near the towns, under the influence of mass media.

Mass media. The 'cultural industry' of mass media inundates Latin America. Only strictly educational and informative programmes have a cultural value. But 'entertainment' programmes have usually a low cultural level and they have a harmful effect on certain fields:
1. The ever growing destruction of the regional cultural elements, which have not sufficient strength to resist such influences.
2. The mistaken indoctrination of youth and the underprivileged sectors of society, which tend to acquire a false cultural varnish through these influences, varnish which follows foreign patterns and has no relationship whatsoever to the Latin American world.
3. The remodelling of Latin American societies in accordance with extraneous values, which bear no relation to the realities and values of Latin America.

These influences result in an apparent cultural progress, which falsifies and alienates Latin American youth from the continent's organic cultural development.

Culture of the élite in Latin America

Elites have a high cultural level, but they have had small success in influencing national societies, caused by:
1. Lack of knowledge and connexion with local situations and problems.
2. Desire to impose foreign patterns, i.e. Europe in the nineteenth century, and Europe and the United States of America in the twentieth century.

The university. It serves only privileged minorities. University education should be urgently extended, to produce large numbers of technicians, scientists and specialists. There is very little planning and co-ordination between universities.

Foreign aid to universities exists in all countries. On the whole, it is helpful. But it has doubtful advantages when it tends to turn the Latin American university into a mere satellite or reflection of a foreign cultural centre.

Scientists and technicians. They frequently tend to emigrate to the United States of America for lack of equally attractive opportunities in their own countries. The paradox of this situation is that the poor countries make presents of their technicians to the rich countries . . . The responsibility of scientists and technicians is that they should accept limited economic conditions and collaborate in Latin American cultural progress. The responsibility of governments is that they must create good working opportunities for their own scientists and technicians.

Creative artists. In this field, there is no underdevelopment. Latin America has great poets, novelists, composers, painters, sculptors, architects, etc.

The relation between artist and public is deficient. Cultural underdevelopment is of course a barrier between creators and the majority of the population. Mass media tend also to use imported programmes, and therefore they neglect the local creators.

The solution to this wrong situation seems to be in the hands of universities. If universities could count on their own mass media elements, they could organize programmes by their own local creators. In this way, the relationship between artist and public would be the normal one. And besides, mass media would really get an organic cultural level, and would make the majority of the population participate in cultural life.

With regard to the prophetic powers of creative artists, the great social and political problems are inescapable. Faced with them, the creative artists adopt decided attitudes.

Such powers should be taken seriously, as artists are the moral conscience of their peoples and often reflect the opinion of large sectors of the population.

Questions on working paper in connexion with mass culture

1. *Is 'mass culture' different in value to 'high culture'?*
   In Latin America, 'mass culture' means in general a very low level of culture. Yet the majority of the population in their rudiments of culture, are more authentic, very often, than the élite.
2. *What has been the offect of an expanding literacy on the creation of and participation in culture?*
   Useful but not complete. If the social stagnation is not ended, literacy tends to become illiteracy again.
3. *What has been the effect of mass-produced books, recordings, radio and television on the right to participate in cultural life?*
   In this respect, mass media have a good effect: they create the conscience in the population that they have a right to participate in cultural life.
4. *To what extent may it be said that mass media cater for the lowest common denominator?*
   If the mass media are commercially designed, they tend to cater for the lowest common denominator. If, on the other hand, they are planned by institutions related to education, like ministries of education, universities, they attain an organic cultural level, according to a planned programme.

33

Discussion

F. Debesa During this part of the discussion I should like to refer to a particular aspect of traditional culture, and the lack of traditional culture in certain countries. Due to the fact that élites have been looking outwards for centuries in some developing countries there has been no knowledge or conscience of our particular traditions in culture. I think, therefore, that the situation in our developing countries is very different from that of the developed countries. When one goes to countries like France or England, one is struck by the way in which traditions are alive; they can be felt everywhere. In our countries, one does not feel them. The reason is that for 300 years the élite has been looking outside, and therefore nothing which has to do with our real roots—Spanish and Indian roots— is either visible or preceptible anywhere. The importance of this should not be underestimated. Because of this neglect of our traditional roots we have no clear sense of identity about ourselves, either as individuals or as communities, and this is particularly serious at the present moment.

Why are television programmes from the United States so dangerous to developing countries? It is because these countries are weak. I wish to be absolutely fair on this and to state it clearly. I never for a moment meant that there was any intention on the part of the United States to cause any damage in these countries. If they are damaged by the United States it is their own fault, because they are lacking in any clear picture of what they really are. Therefore, when something influences them from outside they are not strong enough either to receive it, or to analyse it, or to take advantage of it. The situation is very different in a developed country, to which you can send all the Coca-Cola, all the television programmes you wish from the United States; such a country can take them. It is this question of our weakness that I wish to stress; and, here, I must admit that 90 per cent of this is due to the attitude of our élite over the past 300 years. We have neither a clear picture, nor a consciousness, of what we are, and it is for this reason that we are easily influenced by everything, good or bad. Now, if we could institute some kind of cultural planning which would examine attentively the roots of our culture and thus bring each inhabitant of Latin America to a consciousness of what he is, of what we are—to what extent we are Spanish and to what extent we are Indians—make us realize that we have produced things of great value in the past and that we are still producing things of great value today, this would be real nourishment to us. And this knowledge of our past, of our cultural value, would strengthen us so that we would then be in a position to take what we want, what would enrich us, from the United States or from any other country. I am really confessing our inability to be clearly conscious of what we are, in other words, our lack of tradition. Developing countries have an urgent need for traditional culture.

Y. Cohen I think that one of our basic problems is the whole concept of traditional culture. Tradition is lovely; it reminds us that we must obey our parents, that we cannot completely forget our ancestors, and it also brings into very sharp relief the whole idea of the sanctity of history. Many of us have had drummed into us, in one way or another, that without tradition, without traditional culture, we are lost, we have no identity, we shall be floundering in a sea of the unknown. And we must keep looking to the past, because that is where

34

tradition is. Tradition is past. Here, I think, we have a very good example of some of the things that were mentioned yesterday, namely the colonial roots, or the colonial substructure of much of my own discipline, namely cultural anthropology, which, to a large extent, has been responsible for the respectability of this concept of traditional culture. True, the concept of traditional culture is important, but there is another concept without which the concept of traditional culture becomes meaningless, and that is the idea that there are things in human life, in social organization, in culture, as well as in tradition, that are completely maladaptive to the present conditions under which people live. I think that, once and for all, some public body ought to say that there are times when we are compelled to assert: tradition be damned. I am using the term 'maladaptive' in its original sense, in the Darwinian evolutionary sense. That which is adaptive facilitates the perpetuation of life; that which impedes or does not facilitate the perpetuation of life is maladaptive. And there are times when tradition does impede the perpetuation of human life, its enjoyment, and bringing it to whichever point it is meant to come to. The purpose of life is to perpetuate life, and there are many things in all our traditions, whether they be African, Asian, European, etc., which are maladaptive.

If I may make an issue of what Mr. Debesa just said, yes, it is true that in many areas of South America there is a vacuum when it comes to the question of traditional culture. But, perhaps, we ought also to consider the hypothesis that the search for such a traditional culture might be impeding or might inhibit the entrance of people into the modern world. And, for example, when people say, under the cloak of anthropological respectability, 'You must look for traditional culture', and when most of these voices are heard from outside of the countries involved maybe this is an attempt to keep people out of the mainstream of the modern world. And, although tradition is lovely, especially for the tourist trade, especially for historians, especially for people who have a very good eye for the exotic, for the colourful, for the unusual, perhaps for living people the last thing that they need in this world is traditional culture. And perhaps the first thing that they need is a modern culture.

G. Lamming   It seems to me that this question of tradition, this whether or not you will make this backward glance, is very closely linked with the question of confidence. As a society acquires a certain kind of confidence, the element of controversy about looking back disappears. For example, if you take the United Kingdom, a good example of what you might call tradition is the House of Lords. But the large part of this generation have no doubt in their minds that this thing should go. Now, actually the House of Lords, seen in that sense, belongs to the same level of what is called 'tribal activity'. But neither the old, nor the younger people are disturbed about whether it will have to go or not, because there has been a developed confidence in the society, a confidence about the society's past. Now, I understand Chile's case because one of the sharpest examples of this lack of traditional culture is to be found in the Caribbean. The reason for this is that it is quite unique in the sense that here is a society, or groups of societies, which really only started in any organized sense about 400 years ago. These groups of societies were made up of immigrants from every continent. That is to say that no West Indian there today has any ancestral root in that soil. The only tradition he has is the tradition that has been made by whichever institutions and processes of work (plantations, slavery, to begin with) or whichever kind of social milieu, has been made there. Now, there is a good reason for looking back in a situation like this, not because one wants to invent a culture, but because it has been discovered by responsible educated people and particularly creative artists that very large sectors of the history of the peoples had been removed from the curriculum of learning of the educational system whether past or present. This means that the educational system was largely based on that particular factor of history that seemed to be worth while, in this case, European factor of the islands' history. This also means that at no level of education until very recently was there a curriculum that included any mention of Africa, or Africans, as an occasion for study, in spite of the fact that 90 per cent of the population of those territories have been the descendents of Africa. The reason is that this represented another chunk of the consciousness of society, but a chunk that was not to be brought to the attention of the people who were in the process of learning. We are finding now that tradition is absolutely essential and, as such, it is not of the past at all; it belongs very much, in a way, to the present. There is a necessity for looking back; not in order to invent a cultural mould, or anything like that, but because it is necessary for us to work out, to adjust, and to master our correct relation to that area of our history that was ommitted from the process of learning.

T. Martelanc   I would just like to add something to what Mr. Lamming said. I think that what I am going to say may be a contradiction in itself, but I would like to stress that I view tradition from a dynamic point of view. Personally, I would be reluctant to take a static view of tradition as a cultural phenomena, or as something which is really bound to local indigenous set-ups. I do not think that tradition in Latin America is much confined to Indian tribes. I think that tradition is something which accumulates, something which is also derived from the culture the settlers brought along with them and that today it has become a kind of synthesis. However, tradition exists; it is something which is not only within nations, or within groups, but it is also within us, within every individual. And, as such, it accumulates daily. This is the dynamic point of view I hold on tradition. What is new today becomes tradition tomorrow. Beethoven, in his time, was thought a revolutionary, because he created new values, a musical 'new-look'. But now he is a part of tradition. So are many writers, like Voltaire, for instance, not to mention others. These people, progressive in their time, have become part of the whole cultural heritage of all mankind. I would like therefore to see tradition not only as a social category but also as a historical category. It is not only different from place to place, from group to group, but for each place, for each group, for each individual, it is also different at different stages of time.

B. Breytenbach   Mr. Lamming said: 'Tradition is not just looking back; we *need* to look back'. I would like to complete this phrase by using what is, of course, a theatrical term but which applies in this case: I think that, very often, we need to look back in anger. In this context, I disagree entirely with what Dr. Cohen said, I think we ought to leave this whole concept of cultures being maladaptive or adaptive to one side. Naturally, we have to keep in mind that this phenomenon of cultural imperialism exists in the modern world in which we live today; nevertheless, I do not see how we can define what is adaptive or maladaptive in any given society's culture. Even if we did decide to apply this criteria, who or what is going to be the authority to say whether or not a culture is adaptive or maladaptive? It seems to me that if cultures are not adapted to modern life or are not strong enough to withstand influences from without they will in the end automatically adapt themselves.

K. Aoyagi   What exactly does Dr. Cohen mean when he says that it is important in the modern world to evaluate the adaptive qualities of traditional culture? Dr. Cohen is certainly aware of the fact that tradition gives not only stability and identity, but also creativity. Tradition should be looked upon as a source from which we get our force in order to build a new life, a new indentity, a new stability in creativity.

R. Thapar   We must be clear in our minds that a powerful culture will inevitably influence a weaker culture. That should be absolutely clear to us and we should not waste much time on this. As in a family, as in a nation, as in a caste, this is so. The second point is that the problem before the world is not really one of absorbing modernization. This process goes on at full speed. The problem really is to correct the futile imitation of modernization, a modernization which is being rejected by modern societies. How is this to be done? And the third point, which is absolutely clear to my mind, is that there are aspects of traditional culture which have to be done away with. We are even doing away with them without saying so, because we feel that it offends our humanism to say so. But, in fact, policies of governments in developing countries are designed to break precisely those elements which stand in the way of development. So, I don't think there is so much disagreement between us. Actually, we are working towards an understanding, which will modify our positions as we go along. I would like to give an example which will illustrate these points. In Indian traditional theatre, we are now adopting the most modern forms of mounting scenery. Now, the mere fact that you adopt a modern form, which everyone appreciates, (even the most backward illiterate villager in India appreciates the presentation in a modern dramatic form) the moment you do that you condition the literature of theatre. You condition the entire movement that takes place. You condition the presentation of character on the stage. The whole influence of modern theatre comes into traditional theatre. Take the example of music. We have a music which you can only appreciate if you are prepared to let yourself be intoxicated over six or seven hours. Since time is lacking, because of a modern society which has to sleep at night, a musician is compelled to proceed to a hall where he has to perform his piece within a half hour. Now this fact conditions not only the raga which he is playing, it conditions the instrument. Musicians will tell you that the instrument itself is undergoing a change. To me, this is not a violation of tradition.

The same thing exists in literature, in our traditional forms of literature. People who are writing literature now, because the world is shrinking, learn of the new forms of expression. These are immediately being introduced into the language and they are conditioning the expression of traditional literature.

Take poetry. Indian poetry has always been recited before thousands of people. There is a rapport between audience and poet. I remember when Pablo Naruda was in India this was the great lesson he learned. He recited his Spanish verse to an Indian audience which did not understand Spanish (however, there had been an explanation of what his poem was all about) and there was rapport, and Naruda was thrilled with this experience.

These are examples of the changes in traditional culture in India. There is another side to the question: although it may not be recognized as such, the advanced world has already taken over parts of the culture of the Third World. So much of new European philosophy that is percolating into the world is taken from our Upanishads. But only a few Western writers will admit this source. Now, if they were to admit that source always—and I include the great intellectuals of France in this category—which they say is new it would be seen that the thought was speculated upon in India in the days when there was time to speculate on it. Now this is where the correction has to come, where the two-way pipeline has to be developed. I think that there Unesco has a very vital role.

It is no use imagining that we can, in ten years, build up the strength that advanced countries have built up over centuries. It is not possible. We have to create a climate of opinion, and a climate of opinion is created by a status symbol. Therefore, new status symbols, new value systems have to be consciously propagated. We have to go back and rediscover ourselves within a modern setting. Also I hope that the international organizations, gathering unto themselves the enlightened, will create a two-way system.

Cultural interaction

Cultural interaction

by Breyten Breytenbach

Questioning is questing

No man is uncultured. Article 1 of the Declaration of the Principles of International Cultural Co-operation (Unesco) states: 'Each culture has a dignity and value which must be respected and preserved.' Here, we can substitute the word 'individual' for that of 'culture'.

What is culture? For the individual it is certainly a quest for knowledge, an effort at understanding the unknown, a way of situating himself and probably a way of passing on knowledge (concepts, memories), or just passing on the questioning and the need thereof. It embodies the hopes, the fears, the pride, the joy and the misery of a family or group or community. Seen as a conscious structure it can be (and is) used to expand the power of the community over members of that community or other communities; as a structure it sometimes serves as a nostalgic refuge for the economically weak and the politically disinherited. There can be no criteria to measure and compare various cultures without those criteria being defined by the relative political and economic strength of those cultures.

What is cultural interaction? In the working paper prepared for this meeting by the Secretariat we read: '. . . Culture is the essence of being human'. Being human—to be—is to exist in relation to others, to communicate, react, influence and be influenced—in short: to interact. Interaction is the essence of being human. Therefore, culture is interaction—on an individual, communal, racial, national and international level. Interaction is what cultures do. Interaction is the practice of culture.

I shall therefore look at cultures not as structures (or edifices) but as vehicles of thought and action; not at cultures as they are, but cultures as they do and as they are becoming.

To do the above, and in order to show up the lack, the presence or the necessity of 'rights' in cultures, I shall discuss briefly (a) the right to interact of the individual artist/protagonist/teacher; (b) cultural interaction on the national level, i.e. within the boundaries of one state (and here I shall have to use South Africa as my example, it being the country I know best

39

and also because we are in the presence there of starkly opposed cultures); and (c) cultural interaction on the international level—where we may talk of 'active' and 'passive' cultures and where, as far as the Third World is concerned, it has been rather more of a penetration than an interaction.

(a) There can be no doubt that the most strenuous efforts must be made to protect the cultural rights (the absolute freedom of expression) of the individual, who is the basic cultural unit. The artist, the writer, of our epoch is often living under conditions of intense stress and with a growing sense of alienation and personal frustration (because of a rapidly expanding and industrializing and dehumanizing society). In order to adapt, he is bound to question and contest the structures (cultural and other) of his society, to question and contest the assumptions and the dogmas upon which these structures are based, to question and contest the individuals, instances, groups and interests, who and which benefit from those structures when other groups suffer through them.

This need for protection—and often the absence of any protection—is shown up the moment the individual actively starts to contest and criticize customs, structures, institutions, mores, accepted ideas, etc. It is essential that the individual, the cultural unit, be protected so as to interact freely—and therefore ultimately constructively. This should not be a privilege extended by a permissive society, but an universally accepted and practised right. Cultural action (interaction on the personal level) *is* the constant re-evaluation of existing frameworks.

(b) In the present world—and this is particularly true of South Africa—all culture, literature and art belong to particular classes and to particular political ideas. Art for art's sake, art separated from the class from which it emanates (or the racial group or community), art independent from politics or parallel to it does not in reality exist. Proletarian culture, for example, is part of the whole proletarian revolution; it is, as Lenin put it, 'the nuts and bolts' of the machinery of a revolution as a whole.

Arthur Bryant wrote (in the *Illustrated London News*, 9 July, 1964): 'And since man lives in communities, the test of a community's virtue is the capacity of its institutions and traditions to evoke the spiritual greatness of its members. A community which fails to do this is failing as a community and will in the long run perish, because it will come to consist of men and women who never become what they were intended to be: it will consist, in other words, of human failures.'

This is the case in South Africa where we presently have little or no cultural interaction. There is no cultural interaction precisely because there is a complete denial of the human rights of the non-White majority, let alone the cultural rights. The White minority in power pretends to 'preserve the separate cultures'—which, in practice, means preserving the folk-loric—by eliminating and suppressing all contestation which, through culture, may threaten the existing established order.

It is impossible to evaluate the extent of recent cultural interaction, if any, brought about by the co-habitation of various races over three centuries because not only is all such interaction now forbidden but a conscious effort is made by the White community to destroy that interaction which did take place. This interaction (and mutation towards a greater, more comprehensive culture) can only temporarily be checked, though—it can never be stopped entirely. Already we know that the cultures present in South Africa are themselves products of earlier interaction: Afrikaner culture is essentially the offshoot of a shot-gun marriage between European, Malay and Khoi-Khoin elements; the African South African culture has been profoundly influenced by this resultant White African as well as by European cultures.

Here, remnants of a 'Western' culture will only survive in its positive (i.e. valuable and assimilable) aspects to the extent it can be used by the people to further the cause of freedom and on condition that it is *not* used as an excuse or a means by those now in power to justify their domination.

For culture to interact, to flow freely, in South Africa, the present political hierarchies will have to be abolished. To have any meaning at all, cultural activity in South Africa will be, as it must ultimately be, revolutionary and socialist in the real sense of these concepts so often warped and misused.

(c) Let's face it—we seldom react to the abstract (i.e. ethical) merit or beauty of a culture or of its exponents but to the ideas transported and transplanted by it. Culture (when consciously expounded by a group) is not a matter of kind but of degree and/or the uses and abuses of it.

It seems to me that we have internationally (at least as far as the First and Second Worlds, on the one hand, and the Third World, on the other, are concerned) the same situation we have on a national level in South Africa.

I think the problem lies in the fact that we have here basically two different kinds of societies: that which is expansionist, which needs to 'penetrate' and occupy other cultures and areas, which needs to impose its views of society on others, for which it is necessary economically—or at least according to its own estimation of its economic needs and wants— to exploit foreign markets and peoples, and that 'other', humanist and 'passive' society which seems to content itself with what it finds within itself and at home.

In Africa, for example, culture nearly always stresses the family or the group and the human and humanist elements thereof and the culture is used to maintain these.

In the 'White' world, it would seem that individual achievement is emphasized and wittingly or unwittingly used (but I believe it always does so consciously when in contact with other cultures as in colonial and ex-colonial, but still neo-colonial, areas) either to impose the European view and way of life or to maintain the *status quo* where the settler, or his élitist representative, plays a dominant political and economical role. In this way their culture becomes a tool to penetrate and not to interact—though one may ask whether it is possible to penetrate without interaction—and often the reasoned base justifying the eminent position of its exponents or 'members'.

Nowadays we sometimes see examples of fantastically elaborate international financing used by rich powers to propagate their cultures, their views of 'freedom' and 'un-freedom'. At least since the late 1950s and the early 1960s these efforts have been well camouflaged—in the use of gullible individuals, the ample flow of money to finance publishing for example, in the manoeuvring of national and international agencies—all geared to the massive effort of trying to contain real contestation.

Whereas before we could talk of colonialism as the rape of the Third World, we can now qualify neo-colonialism as the prostitution of this same Third World for the benefit of rich customers.

Internationally, the most influential powers have for a long time reacted as a bloc highly aware of its vested interests, highly skilled at preserving these and using all necessary concepts and organs to promote these. We should be very careful lest international organs reflect only the supposedly 'liberal' ideas of these members.

The Third World, whose only vested interest for so long has been physical survival and whose vested interest for the present and the future must be the freedom of real independence and the freedom to forge revolutionary cultures from old fertilizer and new seed, must take its rightful place on the world scene.

Here, too, we shall have to abolish the existing hierarchies if any free interaction of cultures

41

is to take shape. But it will be of no use to ask for this or even benevolently to legislate internationally to bring this about. There will be a free flow only when the hierarchies of power are abolished or when these hierarchies do not feel their power threatened by free interaction (which is inconceivable).

Human rights in culture—the right to interact, which means the possibility to interact—must on an international level in international agencies and councils be reflected in the proportional presence with the proportional influence and power of the Third World. This is internationally a *sine qua non* for cultural interaction, i.e. the mutual dissemination and receiving (sharing) of education.

Finally, the proof of the value of a culture will not lie in the extent to which it 'coloured' other cultures, but in the extent to which, if it was a 'strong' culture, it allowed other cultures to coexist and fully to share that knowledge (technological and other) upon which its strength was based, or, if a 'weaker' culture (i.e. exploited culture) the way in which it was used to subvert and break the grip of stronger cultures. You will have noticed that in addition to pointing to some of the things cultures have been doing, I have also tried to say what—to my mind—they ought to be doing.

I have written this as a writer and painter and as an activist interested not only in the function of culture as a vehicle for thoughts, but also as a vehicle for social and political change.

Cultural interaction as a factor influencing cultural rights as human rights

by V. Mshvenieradze

The scientific approach to the problem of cultural interaction is determined both by real social processes in the contemporary world and by the tasks posed in official documents of the United Nations and Unesco.

Social, economic, political and ideological processes in the world are closely connected with cultural interaction. There is a wide interinfluence of different cultures. The scientific and technical revolution is often interpreted as something that contradicts man's moral and spiritual make-up. Cultural interaction is concerned with being an effective means to save a man from technological offensive, that 'instrumentalizes' man in the process of 'industrialization and mechanization of the world'.

Problems of 'cultural decolonialization' are widely discussed in countries which have recently won political independence from colonial rule. 'Cultural decolonialization' should lead to revival and extension of cultural human rights.[1]

The Universal Declaration of Human Rights of 1948 points out that 'Everyone, as a

1. Suffice it to say that there appeared special new terms: 'a marginal man' and 'unified African culture'.

member of society . . . is entitled to realization . . . of the economic, social and cultural rights indispensable for his dignity and the free development of his personality'.

A special Unesco document—the Declaration of the Principles of International Cultural Co-operation—is devoted to cultural interaction. It contains many ideas of the first magnitude: '. . . ignorance of the way of life and customs of peoples still presents an obstacle to friendship among the nations, to peaceful co-operation and to the progress of mankind'; 'Nations shall endeavour to develop the various branches of culture side by side and, as far as possible, simultaneously, so as to establish a harmonious balance between technical progress and the intellectual and moral advancement of mankind'; 'Cultural co-operation shall be carried on for the mutual benefit of all the nations practising it'.

We can say that cultural interaction is not only a factor but also is an effect of objective social processes. This cultural interaction takes place in real life. Does it always bring desirable results? What organizational arrangements should be made to maintain the principles which are guarded by Unesco: (a) to strengthen peace; (b) to improve interrelation and friendship among the nations; (c) to develop social and technical progress; (d) to stimulate harmony between the technological progess and moral and intellectual development of mankind; (e) to contribute to the mutual enrichment of cultures; and (f) to stimulate cultural development of each and every individual?

Cultural interaction has, at least, three correlated aspects:
1. Among nations and nationalities within a country.
2. Among the peoples of different countries.
3. Common efforts of all peoples to create human culture common to all mankind.

Each aspect should be dealt with under concrete conditions taking into account at least the following: socio-economic factors, level of social development, the general and specific features of each national culture. It seems of importance to generalize the gained experience of regional and international cultural organizations and positive experience of cultural construction in a number of countries, for example in the U.S.S.R.

Scientific understanding of cultural interaction implies definition and specification of this concept, as well as definition of such concepts as 'culture' and 'cultural rights'. Culture may be defined as the sum total of material and spiritual values, created by man in the process of socio-historical practice and which, in the last analysis, are determined by objective laws of social progress; it is his ability to use these achievements in order to subdue the elemental forces of nature, to solve imminent and urgent problems of social development.

The culture of a given society is determined, in the last run, by socio-economic conditions, by the level of production. Any culture has a relative independence. To consider the relative independence as absolute would lead, as a rule, to two mistakes: (a) a necessary condition is identified with a sufficient one: culture is reduced only to spiritual values. This creates an illusion that the problem of cultural interaction may be solved in a purely theoretical realm, without creation of necessary social, economic and political prerequisites for it; (b) 'cultural relativism' prevents a correct theoretical understanding of the problem, because it cannot reveal the very foundation of spiritual culture.

On the other hand, by emphasizing only the immediate relation of culture to the development of production, i.e. disregarding the complicated character of this very relation and relative *independence* of culture creates another illusion as if the development of production automatically leads to the solution of all problems of culture. This results in rejecting the specific features of culture, discarding the relationship between culture and humanism, the problem of an all-round and harmonious development of an individual.

By 'cultural rights' it seems to me, one should understand the rights of a human being to labour and education, to free and all-round development of his or her personality, to an active participation in creating material and spiritual values as well as using them for further progress of modern civilization. These values also include science—natural, social, medical, etc.—since it is an integral part of culture.

Culture is a social phenomenon resulting from human interaction. It is created not by socially isolated individuals but by the whole of society, by the masses. Every member of society can and must enjoy his or her cultural rights. Though created by the masses, culture may not and cannot be always used for their benefit. This injustice is based on social division of labour. Cultural rights and cultural interaction depend on socio-economic and political structure of society.

Socially significant relationships are the most important form of the manifestation of an individual as a bearer of cultural values. It is a certain social system that creates an objective need for cultural development of an individual, for the use of his or her gifts and abilities, providing similar conditions for all its members without any exception.

There is no one common culture in the world today. A bitter struggle is waged for retaining cultural values and traditions, the rights to cultural benefits, sharpening the problem of cultural interaction. Moreover, the existence of many different national cultures brings the problem of a broad cultural interaction to the fore.

Cultural interaction is a real process of mutual influence and mutual enrichment. This process is based on the objective law of social progress. Cultural interaction contradicts imposing culture, absorbing, devouring or holding back cultural development of another nation.

One should distinguish all-human content and specific national features in any national culture. One of the specific features of the historical process of cultural interaction is the gradual creation of all-human culture, incorporating common democratic elements of national cultures. All-human culture does not exist in its 'pure' form beyond national cultures. On the other hand, any national culture belonging to a particular nation is endowed with common content belonging to everyone. The general exists in and through a particular: the particular being the necessary form of the manifestation of the general, a mode of its existence.

Cultural interaction is a form of manifestation of cultural rights which are part and parcel of human rights. It should not lead to group separatism but on the contrary it should contribute to the strengthening of spiritual communication and cultural unification. It implies: (a) mutual enrichment with all-human cultural content; and (b) deep respect for specific national features of culture of another nation.

Who can really respect the culture of his own nation? Only the one who respects, indeed, other national cultures. Who can really respect his own cultural rights? Only the one who respects, indeed, cultural rights of his fellow earth-man. Every human being should be both culture bearer and active propagandist of human being's cultural rights.

To involve broad masses in using their cultural rights and to create real conditions for it is of utmost importance today. Cultural interaction implies continuity—a combination of growing interest in specific national peculiarities of other peoples' culture with retained cultural heritage of all mankind, and also with due care for it.

The question might arise as to whether cultural interaction would lead to a devouring of one culture by another and to the elimination of unique cultural values. This is a real danger in the contemporary world, which has failed as yet to eradicate aggressive wars from the life of society. It is not always possible to foresee the results of cultural interaction. But all necessary measures should be taken to protect cultural values of mankind from destruction. These values express the very spirit of the past and the present.

Cultural interaction leads to mutual understanding. Activities of Unions of Friendship

Societies, the exchange of cultural delegations, exhibitions of different types, international conferences and trade, tourism and other forms of cultural contacts play a great role in promoting friendship, understanding, trust and cultural co-operation. Mass media play a special role in this respect. They should stimulate and strengthen recognition of cultural rights as human rights.

Discussion

V. Mshvenieradze   I have tried to give a definition of culture and cultural rights in the paper I wrote for the meeting on cultural interaction. In so far as Mr. Breytenbach's paper was on the same subject, I feel that we have many points in common; we have, for example, the same way of posing sub-questions as to the methods and approach to be used in this matter. I fully agree with Mr. Breytenbach when he says that no man is uncultured and when he says that interaction is the essence of being human as long as we do not forget that labour should be mentioned when talking about cultural interaction. With regard to the definition of culture, I should like to make here two preliminary observations: first, culture is the result of man's creative activity in the material and spiritual sphere; it does not fall down from the sky, but is created on earth by human beings; secondly, culture should not be reduced merely to spiritual culture, by which I mean theatre, art, music, etc. Such a limited conception of culture usually leads to a misunderstanding when talking about cultural rights. Culture is the result of the creative activity of peoples, of the masses, and, for this reason, it is necessary to eliminate alienation in order to have culture. I feel that culture should not be divided into 'élite culture' and 'mass culture'; it is, as I defined it in my paper, the sum total of material and spiritual values created by man in the process of socio-historical practice which, in the last analysis, are determined by objective laws of social progress. Culture is the ability to use achievements in order to subdue the elemental forces of nature with a view to solving imminent and urgent problems of social development. In my paper, I tried to define cultural rights as the rights of a human being to labour and education, to the free and all-round development of his or her personality, to an active participation in creating material and spiritual values, as well as in using them for the further progress of modern civilization. I include science in these values, since science is an integral part of culture. Each member of society should be able to enjoy the benefits of cultural achievements. Each member of society should be a culture-user and a culture-bearer, since it is the masses themselves which make culture. These are perfectly natural requirements, and, since this is so, it is necessary that the social division of labour be removed and that alienation, poverty, ignorance, etc., be overcome. I consider that we have now reached a point in history when the elimination of such deterrents to cultural rights is possible. Another essential condition, if all men are to benefit from cultural rights, is to eradicate wars from the life of society, and I feel that we should emphasize this. It is true that war is a kind of interaction, but I would call it an anti-cultural interaction. It seems to me that cultural interaction should imply, in the first place, the mutual enrichment of different cultures and, in the second place, deep respect for the specific national features of culture in other nations. This is an absolute necessity in my opinion.

B. Breytenbach   I am not starting from a set of assumptions, I am far more interested in this whole matter of cultural rights from the point of view of what, in fact, ought to be done. This, of course, includes talking about what has been done, or rather about what has been left undone. I must admit that I feel rather depressed and frustrated by what we've done, or left undone, so far. It suddenly occurred to me that here we are, all of us supposedly cultural experts neatly ensconced in our nice suits and our airconditioned room, while probably at this very moment scores of people, that is to say human beings, are being butchered; while at this very moment, writers, that is to say human beings, are sitting in prisons in many countries; while at this very moment, children are dying of starvation for the cause of a war which doesn't concern them at all. You may say that this has nothing to do with culture; I say that if culture has nothing to do with this, then there is no culture, and we may as well go home. For culture to me is, and must be, a consciousness. We have talked about communication. I sometimes think that we are even worse at receiving signals than we are at so-called communicating them. These masses we want to communicate with so desperately, what do they want from us? The knowledge that there is a university somewhere near where someone they know may go to (with luck)? Do they want to stand around sipping champagne or looking at Picassos? I do not think so. At most, they wish just to eat and not to be shot at. The rest may follow naturally. Are we really seriously suggesting that if we have a few more universities, or renew the present ones, we shall change anything? If we do, we are committing the most cynical sin of all: building up a whitewashed wall of culture over which we propose to peer at the natives. We have not stressed enough the terrible state of inequality existing in the world at the present moment. It is getting worse and not any better. Let us at least try to be conscious of this, let us at the very least, state the absolute necessity to redress some balance before we can even start thinking about our soft culture again. I came across a quotation quite accidentally, written by a friend, an African writer from South Africa called Lewis N'Kosi, in a monthly newsletter called *South Africa Information and Analysis*. I think it sums up perfectly what I am concerned about. He says: 'This is one of the deepest weaknesses of Western democracies' (and although he probably does not mean this I should like to enlarge this to nearly every country excluding the Third World) '. . . The deepest weakness of Western democracies is to invariably confuse law and order with legitimacy, to prefer stability to the unknown consequences of radical change.' And it seems to me that what we have really talked about here is the way cultures react when in the presence of something foreign to them, in the presence of a foreign culture. This reaction, it seems, would take one of two forms: either to fall back on old cultures, or at least its most obvious characteristics, that is, its language or its religion, for example; or it tends to become even more bastardized, taking over large chunks of the culture by which it has been dominated. It is only normal that an oppressed people should try to incorporate those elements of the foreign culture to which its strength may be ascribed. The attitude of the exporting powers, that is the powers which have the strength, the ability or the aptitude to export not only what they have to sell but what they want others to buy should be, are our ideas the ones they want to buy? What I call the exporting powers have been trying to sell their ways of life, lock, stock and barrel. I think this is borne out by the very notion, for example, of democracy, or, for that matter, the very notion of social sciences. We judge new national States by their degree of democracy. We judge new States coming into existence in Africa, in Latin America, in Asia, by standards which are Western in essence. We ascribe a certain value to them, to the degree to which they conform to the Western standards. Can we, in the Third World, assimilate the technological and scientific material which we need to be able to affirm or to reaffirm ourselves internationally (or even just to maintain ourselves), without having to assimilate everything, without becoming cultural satellites? I, myself, find this prospect very exciting.

There is such a thing, I think, as cultural shame. We need to affirm ourselves again, we need to build, to create, and to rid ourselves of this shame. In South Africa this is particularly the case. Here we are assisting at the moulding of a vigorous new culture because it takes place within a framework of difficult struggle. As the struggle continues we shall, I think, quite naturally work out the élite. Once one is a cultural élitist, one is nearly automatically a political élitist. The contestation of political élitism, that is the contestation of the settler, or the representative from elsewhere, leads to a cultural contestation. Contestation is for me absolutely essential, on three different levels: the personal, the national and the international level. On a personal level, I think it is becoming impossible for the creative artist, for the writer, for example, not to take note of the mass struggle. On the international level—and this is probably why we are here—the only right we should preserve, since we talk about human rights, is really the right to equality. However, this right does not exist and it is no use pretending that it does. It can only exist once there is really equality of opportunity, or representation in the international organs, be they cultural, political, economic or anything else. It would be an illusion to talk of cultural equality as long as the other forms of equality do not exist. Nor can I see how this can come about without a contestation of the present balance of power, the present 'rapport des forces', as it exists in the world. As long as we do not have this equality, two-thirds of the world is going to be waste for exploitation, as it is now. It will remain as it is and we shall go deeper into shame, degradation and indignity. If it is necessary to burn what already exists in order to re-establish some form of equality which will represent us internationally as we ought to be represented internationally, then we must burn, even if it means burning the whole lot down. I am not making a case for violence; I am merely stating that this particular choice is being imposed upon us increasingly, and it is dangerous.

G. Lamming   The inequality that you are speaking of between what you call rich and poor nations does not only exist between rich and poor nations. It can exist within the same country. We are already involved not only in the business of the deprivation of the rights that make for cultural diffusion, but it seems, at this stage, of the impossibility of these rights. In my part of the world, it seems to anyone who is a creative artist, whose principal duty is authenticity of expression, that is the authenticity of expression that reveals the integrity of his response to life, that political rights are the prerequisite for cultural rights.

R. Thapar   Every revolution has imagined that it was going to unleash a radical culture, and it has ended up enchained again. Unless we change our terms of reference, unless we attack the value system consciously, not by a brain-washing but by a brain-cleaning operation, I do not think we are getting anywhere.

N. Otieno   It is going to prove more and more impossible, I think, to preserve separate cultures. In the light of what is happening today in the twentieth century (somebody said this morning that the transistor is there for the asking) you cannot really preserve some of the separate cultures. The word 'mutation' was used in connexion with the interaction of cultures, and I find this particularly interesting. When an organism mutates it is undergoing changes within itself, changes over which it has no control. It is being governed and necessitated by forces from without. And if you apply the word mutation to portray interaction, the interaction will not only be on the cultural and human individual level but will also be affected by extraneous forces over which you and I have no control. This is where the application of science and technology comes in. And this is where, I think, protection becomes difficult. Look at society as an organism; when it starts to mutate there is no control.

You talk about hierarchies in South Africa, and here I refer to hierarchies anywhere in the world. I think events are against them. Whether you want it or not cultural interaction is going to take place. You may be repressive, you may try to use educative influences to get your populations, or societies, or groups to follow what you want them to follow, but culture is ever evolving and within the modern world of today I do not think any régime is going to succeed in trying to isolate individuals from acquiring and mutating, while interacting with each other. While you are penetrating into another culture you are wittingly or unwittingly absorbing what you think you are penetrating into.

V. Mshvenieradze   It is quite impossible to set up barriers because even if you wish to set up barriers and isolate a country, you will fail. As you know, ideas fortunately do not need visas and passports to go abroad, so cultural interaction is a fact. As far as we are concerned, I think we should do our utmost to promote the positive sides of cultural interaction. Professor Otieno put a very interesting question about the preservation of culture. He said: 'If one emphasizes the need for preservation, then one cannot say that there is a constant re-evaluation of existing frameworks'. This is true. At the same time, I would like to point out here a very interesting and rather difficult problem. The fact is that no culture germinates in pure ground, and in cultural interaction as well as in cultural development, there is always continuity. National culture has within it elements of international culture. The question has been asked: 'Where are these elements of international culture and where are these elements of national culture? What should we support, and what should we not support?' I think that this is an objective process. The objective criteria of what should be accepted is social progress. If it promotes social progress, then it is positive and it should be accepted and supported. If not, then it should not be accepted.

R. Thapar   I should just like to add to the points that were raised on the question of rich and poor nations, rich and poor peoples; of élites, largely rich, assuming their culture from outside and projecting it as a status symbol inside their countries. This is even happening to those who talk of traditional culture. This is happening throughout the developing world, and as the economic, political and military systems of developing countries become more involved with the more powerful cultures, that influence is reflected more forcefully in the national life of each developing country. And the political impact of this is the polarization of the élite from the mass, which, in turn, leads to a movement which is insular. It sets up the barriers against the entry of foreign culture, under the slogans of extreme nationalism. This we are also witnessing in the developing world, and we know the consequences of it. Obviously, if we are going to be at all relevant to this crisis of our time we have got to move towards some understanding of what we intend to do about it. To me, that is the content of cultural rights. I think we should really concentrate our discussion on what we feel should be done about it.

There is a field of culture which is being eroded: national cultures are being eroded by the powerful cultures, which are moving in. And I believe that they are basically on the plane of industry, technology and science. These fields influence the way of life of a whole people when they are developing. However, I want to go back to what we were discussing earlier. Can we demarcate the sectors of culture? Is there a culture which is inevitable, which will destroy certain traditional cultures in the whole process of development? That culture which is universal, it has come, it has arrived. Is there a relevant national culture which will live for all time? And what will happen to the sub-cultures? Do they also have a content which will live, or will they be destroyed? I think that unless we break culture down, unless we stop looking at it as one big term, as one whole area, we are not going to get anywhere, because, in fact, we are already witnessing the destruction of cultures all around the world. And we have to decide on what is a good, progressive destruction, what is renewable, and what is not. That is where shame comes in.

Y. Cohen   I should like to ask what it is we are referring to when we talk about swallowing cultures, either swallowing parts of cultures, or giving back some of it.

G. Lamming   I do not think, again speaking with specific reference to the Caribbean area, that the issue is fear of exposure, the issue is not fear that one might be swallowed up. The real issue in the experience of people of my generation and younger is: we do not know how, in the total political and economic circumstances we can make communication a two-way process. At the moment, communication between North America and the rest of America is a one-way communication. It is not a two-way communication. We would like a two-way communication. One would like a genuine and authentic dialogue to take place with Americans who want to know what is the reality of our existence. We are not connected by the structure of the society to those pipelines of power which give our voices an utterance. If you can find a way to introduce into this communication a genuine reciprocity of exchange, it would be acceptable to us.

Y. Cohen   Someone said that we had to start attacking the values. I would suggest that perhaps it is not the values that we have to attack, or the values that have to be questioned, but rather the whatever it is that keeps particular value systems going. People can attack the values until they are blue in the face. There is always the foundation which underlies them. Unless this is changed or moved, then the values are going to remain. Finally, what I would like to suggest is that maybe one of the things we should talk about is the role of dominant military groups. Perhaps one of the most fundamental human rights we can talk about in terms of this interpenetration of cultures by each other is the preservation of a system whereby 1 or 2 per cent of the population in a society controls the sources of energy of that society and preserves it in other countries as well.

R. Thapar   I do not think there is any difference, because when you attack the value systems you attack the institutions behind them. You cannot attack the value system in a vacuum.

Some problems outlined

Social role of writers

by George Lamming

I would like you to consider all the implications of the following piece of dialogue:

Question: Why don't you work?
Answer: Because I am not a worker.

Question: What are you?
Answer: I am an artist; a writer to be exact.

Question: But what do you do?
Answer: I write.

Question: I see. In long hand or short hand?
Answer: I type.

Question: I see. You are a typist.
Answer: You don't understand. Goodbye.

There are societies of relatively high practical literacy in which such a conversation, brief and sometimes turbulent, can take place any morning. The social role of an artist or writer in such a society would be to work for the creation of an ambience, an atmosphere of mutual awareness which would make such dialogue impossible.

This will not apply to societies with prosperous economies and a long tradition of indigenous culture created by members of an educated class who have always regarded artistic activity as a natural and essential mode of rendering human experience.

But the society I have in mind—the English-speaking Caribbean—presents a certain paradox. It is modern in the sense that it is part of a major language of civilization and uses all the technical tools of survival and communication which are to be found in the modern world. At the same time it has had a history—slavery and colonialism—which was dedicated

51

primarily to the creation of wealth for an external power; a history which always worked against the creation of culture as an expression of the people whose work and general experience made for a particular social milieu.

If we consider seriously the fragment of dialogue above, we shall see that the questions are, in substance, sound and just. Why don't you work? What do you do? What are you? These are sound and just questions because they tell us, honestly, something about the society's concept of work by selecting a particular category of human activity which the society regards as non-work.

The answers, on the other hand, are defensive and less illuminating; and the final accusation, 'You don't understand', is in the nature of an evasion. It is an attempt to close the subject which—as the writer himself knows—remains open and very urgent for any one who is concerned with transforming the education and values of such a society.

The writer or artist is, in fact, a citizen and a worker; and his social role should be contained in the process of that work. The novelist or poet in such a society would be performing a social role of the greatest importance by writing the novels and poems which he feels he has to write and which bear witness to the experience of that society at any or all of its levels. A social function has truly been fulfilled if such work helps to create an awareness of society which did not exist before; or to inform and enrich an awareness which was not yet deeply felt.

The rights to culture would demand that such a society should not be deprived of those citizens who do such work. The rights to culture would demand—in the sense of expect and urge—that such a society should be free to achieve a dialogue of mutual awareness between itself and those workers—novelists, poets, painters, etc.—whose social role is to be seen in the very nature and process of their work: they return the society to those areas of experience which remain largely invisible between citizen and citizen in the normal course of living together. They return the society to itself: to its past as well as to those visions of a future which constitute its present.

The English-speaking Caribbean—a post-colonial society whatever the political constitution of the particular island territory may be—offers an example of the kind of deprivation which makes mutual awareness almost impossible between the society and its cultural workers. This deprivation appears in three ways. The first has to do with the mass of the people. They represent a pool of labour historically alienated from their own experience and culture by barriers of literacy. This was a deliberate policy of the educational system. The second aspect of deprivation is to be seen in the isolation of the cultural worker (novelist or poet, etc.) by a native minority middle-class whose tastes and interests are hostile to the values which define an artist's work. This group is very important since it represents the technical and administrative brain power of the society. It is an example of the native intelligence as a product of foreign tutelage. Its power has no real basis in the economy although its members are prosperous, but its influence, which derives from its professional training and skills, is very considerable. The third way in which deprivation manifests itself is in the relation of the official administration to all forms of mass communication. There is a nervousness, an acute hypersensitivity to the kind of creative inquiry which is the very basis of art. This reaction is logical in areas where unemployment is high and social and economic frustration is the prevailing characteristic of the young.

What can the writer or artist do in these circumstances? Let us begin with what many have done. In a recent collection of critical essays on West Indian literature published by the Oxford University Press there is a bibliography of the work mentioned: the fiction is represented by some 65 novels written mainly over the past 15 years by about 20 novelists. About

16 of these writers are now resident outside of the Caribbean: either in the United Kingdom or the United States. More than 50 of the 65 books would have been written abroad. They are largely unavailable to the West Indian populations: to the people whose lives and whose societies are, in fact, the raw material, the fuel power of the fiction itself. It is very likely that such an example has many parallels in other places; and it would be interesting to compare the patterns of experience wherever such a situation obtains.

It is impossible to over-estimate the value of those writers and artists who, whatever the reason, have continued to work and live in this situation where the rights to culture remain severely impeded by the legacy of economic and psychological dependence on one external power or another.

The social role of writers and artists will extend, of course, to other activities than the immediate practice of writing novels and poems. As a citizen and a worker, he shares in the general impulse to transform any system which threatens him with deprivation of any kind. He fulfils a social function whenever he joins forces with any pressure group whose hunger for free creative expression is the same as his, although their work may take some form other than writing.

Deprivation of the rights to culture may take a variety of forms including the gift of culture itself. One example of this is the function of television in some poor and independent territories of the English-speaking Caribbean. There is a tendency to feel disgracefully impoverished if you are independent and without this very sophisticated medium of communication. In fact, it serves, in some new independent states, as the latest and most effective instrument of deprivation, for it consolidates the very impoverishment which authentic communication is intended to abolish. It prolongs the tradition of foreign tutelage by offering a content of human experience which is not only spurious in itself, but utterly irrelevant to the needs and experience of the society on which it is imposed as a criterion for arriving at modernity.

West Indian society started as an experiment in the creation of wealth for the colonizing powers of the time.

> The world's green age was then a rotting lime
> Whose stench became the charnel galleon's text.
> The rot remains with us, the men are gone.

> (From *Ruins of a Great House*, Derek Walcott.)

The social role of the writer and artist, in these circumstances, is to help cleanse the society of 'this leprosy of empire' which persists, will not let go, goes into hiding only to return with new races and more subtle briberies.

Discussion

G. Lamming   I should like to make some observations about the use of European languages by many non-European writers. There is a certain contradiction in the fact that African writers, for example, have to write in a language which is not their own, whereas they are attempting today to report their experience in fiction. This reporting of their experience should normally be considered as part and parcel of a growing desire to redeem the original language, to get back to the very roots of their culture, and it is this conception which has made one brand of nationalists criticize strongly certain writers for using what they term 'the enemy's tools' in order to project themselves. It seems to me that the choice of a European language by an African writer raises not so much a contradiction as a fusion. If you examine the content of many African novels, you will find that two worlds are co-existing. Their entire content deals with the very formal structure of African living, and this is crystallized and rendered in a foreign language. In my opinion, this fusion, which enables two situations to co-exist, does not constitute a contradiction, in the sense that it is not an obstacle. It may well be that there is a desire in the developing world to return to tradition, but because of the infinite power and range of mass communication it is no longer really possibile for anything that you call the developing world to develop at all without pressure and influence from that other world. The extraordinary cultural monopoly held by the developed world does not allow for any development of an isolated traditional culture. It does not allow for that rigid compact mentalization of development by either the developing or the developed worlds.

R. Thapar   This feature of writing in the language which is the 'enemy's', as you call it, is a feature which is characterizing literature throughout the developing world, and it is not really a question of finding a bridge across by which one can attain a wider audience. It is, in fact, connected to your second point: the cultural monopoly held so rigidly in certain areas persuades the creative writer to attempt work in a European language, because he gets more reward and more recognition by doing so.

B. Breytenbach   There is another problem: when coming from the developing world one tends to write in English or French because it conforms. It goes even deeper than that, probably. If one is a writer or an artist in the developing world, one consciously or unconsciously conforms to an age in which what the writer or artist should do is imposed upon him by the developed world because of this cultural monopoly it exercises. The question has been asked whether the individual creative artist can be protected in a society which is in a constant state of contestation. I do not know the answer, but I feel that it is absolutely essential that all efforts should be made to protect the individual creative artist who, by nature of what he does, will be contesting certain conceptions and certain structures which have been passed down to him or by which he feels himself surrounded. Here I am talking about the person who may go farther than the invisible line which is nearly always drawn by society. In most countries you may contest this or that, but when you get down to the roots of the structures which you are contesting, in other words when this becomes not only a cultural contestation but implies a political contestation, you will be muffled or choked culturally. In South Africa there is no possibility for writers like Alan Paton to publish their novels, because although their works have to do with fictional situations they very often, by their general implications, threaten the power structure of the society. It must be made possible even for someone whom the society may consider renegade in his thinking and in his writing to exist.

F. Jeanson   I would like to express my full agreement with what Mr. Breytenbach has just said. Strange as it may seem, as I listened to him I kept thinking of Burgundy, despite the numerous and tragic differences between the two regions. I mean by this that, as I see it, there are a great many developing countries scattered throught the world, and we all have, as it were, a series of extra Third Worlds to which we have to devote very careful attention. I think we should not allow ourselves to be misled by the absence—maybe only temporary— of a certain type of oppression, repression and violence. Sometimes hidden violence can be just as serious as outbursts of overt violence. Objective forms of violence resulting from systems which proceed under their own force of inertia can be just as menacing for man, for his future development and for his inherent possibility of continually reinventing himself, as acts of violence carried out by such-and-such a régime for the specific purpose of maintaining itself in power. As one travels through a European country, to all appearances 'developed', it is not impossible to discover similar phenomena to those Mr. Breytenbach has mentioned. Personally, I consider that in certain European countries people are living in a world which has fallen to pieces around them. I mean by that that you have, on the one hand, a minority of people in possession of what they call culture (and because they posses it they cannot imagine the existence of other kinds), and, on the other hand, the vast majority of people who are shut out from this culture. Naturally enough, this corresponds in most cases to a deprivation of another sort—an economic deprivation.

It seems to me that we should give our closest attention to this state of affairs, for it is something which threatens us all and, in the last resort, such deprivation is as damaging to us, who are on one side of the fence, as it is to those who are on the other side of it Because of it, we are all, pell-mell, swept onwards towards the same abyss. What strikes me is that, for the most part, everything goes on quite naturally and without serious incidents. For example, it is a fact that we all—all of us—benefit from the process of world-participation: by that I mean that we can all hear every day what is going on in every part of the world. In concrete terms this means that we are opened up, that we are in a permanent state of being opened up to the four corners of the world, and are invited hour by hour, through information reports flashed to us, to take an, to all intents and purposes, identical interest in the serious situation in Hanoi or Biafra and in what is happening in the Forest of Clamart, for instance, where the police are on the lookout for a sexual maniac.

Actually, I believe this over-information that we are supposed to benefit from is nothing short of a catastrophe for us, since we are no longer even able to sift the information supplied to us, and, what is much worse, because we are continually invited to view all such information against one common background which is that of blackmail by the atom bomb. This produces in the people of over-developed countries a feeling of frustration, for they have the impression that anything of decisive importance in the world escapes them completely, is forever outside their range, and that decisions are invariably taken by other people. They are hedged in by a feeling of impotence, for, in fact, they are nowhere at all: they are obviously not in the four corners of the world, to which they are ceaselessly projecting themselves in imagination, nor are they where they ought to be, that is to say, in their own village, their own quarter, their own town, their own district. The feeling, the conviction which every man ought to possess, it seems to me, that he can do something to change the situation, no longer exists. I am convinced that we have all more or less lost that feeling; at any rate, it has certainly been effectively lost by the great majority of our contemporaries Furthermore, the situation is aggravated by the fact that they speak (and we, of course, with them) a language that has lost much of its meaning, that ends by talking to itself, through us as mediums. Communication is well nigh dead, and that seems to me extremely grave. We know quite well that, actually in the case of the great majority of us, we are totally incapable of exerting the slightest influence on the course of events. This history that is being made is not our history; it is a history that is fashioned out of us, nourished by us, but is made in spite of us.

So I think that if culture is to have any meaning at all, it can only be to the extent to which it puts men back, progressively, in the position of being able to feel effective, of feeling responsible in the place where they happen to be, in the light of an information system which remains necessary but which itself needs to be overhauled from top to bottom. My view is that culture begins with reading the newspaper; when our contemporaries can manage to read their daily paper without being utterly mystified or without setting out with the idea that everything they are going to read is a pack of lies—then a definite change will have been brought about. Another definite change that will have been brought about will be when they are in the position of being able to exercise control over the language passing through them as mediums. How are we to set about reaching such a situation? That is something which, I think, we ought to ask ourselves. I feel very strongly that as soon as possible an active content ought to be injected into the notion of 'rights'. Two methods of action are possible in connexion with rights: there is the type of action which consists of trying to have theoretical rights officially recognized, and another type which consists of trying to turn these rights into realities, perhaps even before they have been incorporated in official texts. My point is that, unless both types of action are carried out simultaneously, the chances are that nothing will be done at all. Personally, I would rather speak of culture in terms of cultural action, because in this context a pratical significance is attached thereto; but I would like to say also that this obviously presupposes a certain concept of culture which does not, perhaps, exactly correspond to the one hitherto the most widely accepted. In other words, culture can be regarded either as the totality of existing works or existing forms of expression, or else as something which is happening every day, taking place continually, making and unmaking itself daily at the ordinary level of concrete human intercourse. At every moment everywhere culture is, of course, in process of being made or unmade, as the case may be. I mean by this that culture has to be a permanent, daily reinvention of man by man, and that this reinvention need not necessarily take place. Culture is the perpetual creation of values which are born only to be superseded. A cultural act is, in the last resort, a solemn and even risky decision implying a total engagement of the individual conscience concerned. Culture is a choice carrying with it the refusal to accept that man is a man-produced product. It seems to me this is the attitude we must encourage with every means at our disposal. But here we are brought up against the all-important question—that of the right means for furthering cultural action in this sense, if it is, indeed, in this sense and at this very humble level that we ought to operate. I would add that this amounts to a venture, in the best sense of the word, aimed at arousing in people a profound political consciousness. I do not mean by this that one should try to palm off on people some particular political nostrum or other—far from it! But people must be given the opportunity to become politically minded, in other words ever more and more consciously engaged in choosing for themselves, in situating themselves in the midst of a world which is not yet theirs but which must as quickly as possible become so, if we really want the world to be our world. It will have to be their world and ours at the same time. In this respect I believe that culture—or what I call cultural action—is a venture which is based on a refusal: the refusal to accept a certain exclusion, a certain alienation. This by no means implies any attempt to camouflage the economic causes of such an exclusion; but these must be fought with political weapons.

It seems to me that here a specifically cultural approach is called for, aimed not at disguising the state of economic alienation but at placing men, on either side, in the position of being able to reflect on this situation, of choosing where they stand with regard to it. Although the situations in our respective countries do not yet appear to have become revolutionary situations, we ought nevertheless to concern ourselves seriously with revolution; for if one day they were to become such, at the structural level and that of objective phenomena, the danger is that true revolutionary minds might not be on hand to take charge of them at the crucial moment. My personal view is, however, that we are all whoever we are moving towards explosive situations, revolutionary situations; and so we ought all to prepare ourselves beforehand and have some idea of how best to deal with them. We must see to it that it is not just a small minority of us which has the necessary means of concerning itself with this problem; these means must be placed within the reach of all as quickly as possible. This can only come about gradually, of course, step by step, stage by stage, because we don't yet dispose of the necessary means for going quickly. Yet that is the dilemma we are confronted with: we just have to go quickly, all the same.

To sum up, it seems to me that when we speak of cultural rights we must place considerable emphasis on the task implied by this refusal to accept exclusion, and we may be certain that such a task in no way rules out fighting. And, if fighting there has to be, a dialogue must be engaged in at the same time. That, to my mind is what culture stands for.

T. Martelanc   While listening to Mr. Jeanson it occurred to me that we might add to our final statement a phrase to the effect that the right to culture is not only the right to enjoy cultural benefits and to create actively, but that it is also the right to influence the creators and, in certain cases, also the right to influence the media which transmit culture. I feel that we should include this because creation, whatever form it may take, is not creation in itself; it is also realization. J. P. Sartre has said that the reader is the co-producer of the writer. I think that this right to influence creation, and especially those who transmit cultural benefits, should be one of the basic rights to culture.

F. Debesa   I do not know whether I understood clearly what Dr. Martelanc was saying, but if he is suggesting that the creators should be influenced I would be very much opposed to such an inclusion in our statement. Creators should be left alone to create; to influence them would be very dangerous from every point of view. When they create freely they can perform miracles; as soon as they are influenced, they become mediocre.

F. Jeanson   I understand what Mr. Debesa has just said about creators' need of freedom to create. Nevertheless, I think that creators also need to be placed in contact with those on behalf of whom they purport to create. In France, creators themselves are beginning to realize that they are cut off from the rest of the population, and a movement is already under way for bringing the two closer together. These creators have their public, indeed; unfortunately, it is always the same public. They are marking time, because they are the prisoners of that particular public. Furthermore, there are all those whom I call, personally, the non-public—that is, all the others. The creator is beginning to feel the need to find points of contact, establish relations with this non-public. Don't let us imagine this is out of idealism. The creator's primary motive if, for example, he is a playwright is obviously to make sure that his theatre is filled, that he plays to full house. If the theatre is nearly empty he must look for more playgoers. But this is a primary motive only. In France, at the present time, creators have reached the second phase, which consists of realizing that the problem is more serious, more profound than the mere fact of an empty theatre. Lowering prices of admission and better advertising are no solution. That has nothing to do with it. The fact is that playwrights can no longer afford to act on the basis of a public which remains invariably the same, and to assume that any others who may come will necessarily belong to the same social stratum; they can no longer afford to cater for such a limited social category. Jean Vilar said recently: 'Ever since we started working for theatrical decentralization in France, ever since we started producing a people's theatre, we have never yet managed to penetrate below the lower middle class. There are no workers, no working men among our audience; we have never been able to reach them'. I think it would not be worth while asking ourselves these questions on the subject of culture if we failed to see the vital importance and over-riding urgency of the words just quoted. We shall never get anywhere unless we face this urgent situation directly.

N. Otieno The freedom of the creator depends upon the material he is creating with, and the audience he reaches also depends upon the material he uses. A biologist, for instance, creates as he wishes, and although the people for whom he creates consume his goods he is not dependent upon them for his living. Were he to be dependent upon them for his living he would have to pay attention to their desires.

B. Boutros-Ghali We ought not to forget, perhaps, the role of the popularizer (for, after all, creators are few and far between) who will serve as middleman in our society of the future. You could, therefore, leave the creators their freedom or ivory tower since the popularizer will be there to act as intermediary between them and the public.

Y. Cohen When we talk about the products of creators, such as literature, art, poetry, music and so on, I think we are really talking about creating the conditions that would make it possible for people to relate that which goes beyond their own immediate personal anxieties to a canvas, or a printed page, to music, or to what they see on a television screen or hear on a radio. We know that the hungrier people are the less they can create and the less they can respond to creativity. It is only when we are no longer simply concerned with staying alive that we can start talking about training an audience. At present, for billions of people in the world, the whole concept of controlling one's destiny is a fantasy. I think we are really saying: How do we create the conditions that would make it possible for people to be concerned about their society, their culture, other societies, other cultures?

F. Jeanson A distinction has to be drawn between the various forms of creations from the point of view of progression itself in the matter of culture. The more collective the form of a creation is, the more likely it is to stand in need of taking into account the demands of the collectivity. There are number of writers, for example, who in theory think that one should write for everybody, but who none the less continue to write for themselves, for a handful of initiated. This is much harder for a playwright to do because the theatre is already *per se* a collective art form. I mean that it calls for the services of a group, a team.

Someone spoke of popularizers just now. Personally, I prefer the term 'mediators'. It is a question of creating suitable conditions for placing works of art and men in contact with each other, no matter who or what these men may be, including those for whom, at the present moment, works of art mean nothing at all: that is the situation. If Shakespeare is put on television, people switch off or turn to another programme, because Shakespeare doesn't concern them. That's the whole point: they're not concerned! As long as they refuse to be concerned, it is useless to try to put Shakespeare in the forefront. What we must do is attend to the interests of those who are not concerned with Shakespeare and discover the mediatory art forms suitable in their case. That is what can be called cultural action. We must at all costs manage to get inside the skin of this non-public and get to know it, understand exactly what its problems are, and place ourselves at its service. Cultural action means placing ourselves at the service of this non-public to help it formulate the problems which are its problems, and not the problems which are ours.

F. Debesa   Latin America has given birth to really great creative artists who are being accepted and recognized all over the world today. However, the structures of the countries of this continent are such that the relationship between the creators and what should be their public is practically non-existent. In a way, it can be said that they create in a vacuum. This is related to another factor: cultural invasion. Because the majorities of the population are receiving so much from the outside and so little from the inside the balance between the two is lost. Of course, if we did not have our own creative artists we would have to more or less accept this state of affairs; however, Latin America does have its own creative artists, and one of the urgent tasks in that continent is therefore to create a good and efficient relationship between them and the public, that is to say the majorities of the population. There are many ways in which this problem could be approached. I may appear to have an obsession as far as universities are concerned, but I do feel that here again they could provide this very essential link between the two. If the universities were to have the mass media at their disposal, and this is not at all impossible in my opinion, they could turn to the creative artists to provide books for editing houses, programmes for radio and television, etc. What is needed is to get the creative artists into the public eye; once they have become known in their own countries, the danger from outside influences would not be so great.

A country which is culturally strong can withstand foreign influences. A particular aspect of creative artists is related to their attidudes towards socio-political problems. These problems are so important in Latin America that creative artists have very defined attitudes and opinions with regard to them. In Latin America, intellectuals are not given very much importance, with the exception of a few outstanding examples. Most of them are considered as quaint people who have no practical ideas. People are quite happy that they should write their poems, or paint their paintings, but they do not consider that what these creative artists say about social or political problems merits much attention. This is mainly due to the fact that in the past they where very amateurish in such matters, and they really lived in the ivory towers they had built around themselves. However, for the past ten years they have been much more in contact with the people ('le peuple') and their opinions now reflect this. Their views on such problems should be taken into account seriously.

R. Thapar   One of the questions that could be asked, and which emerges from your paper after reading it, is whether the universities themselves are really the cradles of the élite. You have referred to the fact that so much of the creative work done in Latin America is done in a kind of vacuum; this means, in fact, that the creative artists are serving a market beyond their own, and that they are recognized beyond their own national market. This is a problem which I think applies to a large portion of the developing world. However, you raise a very important point when you say that they are becoming increasingly involved with their own systems. I find that in many developing countries the role of the intellectuals is beginning to be stressed by governments, whether liberal or otherwise. This is an aspect we should go into more deeply.

Rights to culture
from the aspects of mass media

by Tomo Martelanc

The Preamble of the Declaration of the Principles of International Cultural Co-operation[1] recalls 'that the wide diffusion of culture and the education of humanity for justice and liberty and peace are indispensable to the dignity of man and constitute a sacred duty which all the nations must fulfil in a spirit of mutual assistance and concern'. The essence of the role and responsibility for the social function of mass media in the realization of rights to culture is included in this context.[2]

Mass media are conquering the whole world, they are also advancing to remote areas of the world, and sow the seed of social changes. Isolation is practically impossible nowadays. As a means of political and economic propaganda, as a vehicle of cultural exchange and, above all, as an indispensable means for the socialization of man, mass media have become a real social power.

The exposure of man to the activity of mass media and at the same time man's dependence upon it is achieving unforeseen dimensions. Mass communication does not fill only man's free time, it does not mediate only entertainment, information, but eventually it also creatively influences man's thinking, his attitude to life and his behaviour.

This demands a great responsibility for activity and management of mass media. An over-all expansion and a great potential power of these media make possible the dangers of their misuse, when certain ideas can be deliberately introduced to the public, and values can be formed which are not in the common interest and which do not serve human aims, peace and co-operation with other cultures, nations and societies.

The role and activity of mass communication media depend upon the social relations in

1. See: *Records of the General Conference, Fourteenth Session, Paris, 1966—Resolutions*, p. 86–7, Paris, Unesco, 1967.
2. The expression 'mass' when speaking of mass media is not identical with the same expression when used in connexion with 'mass culture'. It is true that culture achieves, thanks to mass media, mass, or 'universal character' (Bauman Zygmunt). The differentiation of culture on 'élitist' and 'mass' culture is rather formalistic, because mass media transmit both the products of 'high' as well as of 'mass' culture. Therefore, it is only possible to speak of culture and about the role which mass media have in spreading it.

which these media operate. Mass communication media do not operate in a vacuum but in the centre of the system of social interactions and among social elements that are linked together and mutually dependent. Thus mass communication media are shaped by the society and vice versa; media influence it through their interpretation of life.

The Universal Declaration of Human Rights states that 'everyone has the right freely to participate in the cultural life of the community to enjoy the arts and to share in scientific advancement and its benefits'. Rights declared in such a way can remain only a dead letter on a piece of paper if we do not create the necessary conditions—social, economic, political, educational—for their realization. This can come true only in the process of the democratization of culture, that is to say, in the endeavour to make cultural benefits available to really broad masses of people.

Cultural and technological advancement, especially under the influence of mass media, contributes in a large degree to the increase of interest in culture, especially among strata to which not so long ago cultural benefits were not accessible. What at one time used to be the domain and privilege of the educated aristocracy is becoming now a means of intellectual and spiritual development for the masses. We witness on the one side higher and higher specialization of cultural activities, and on the other, a larger and larger diffusion of cultural benefits. With this there are created new social dimensions of culture.

Regardless of the disputable theories concerning the importance and function of 'mass culture', it is becoming an incontestable fact that in the contemporary, technologically developed society the circle of 'consumers' of cultural benefits is constantly increasing and that in this process of the democratization of culture mass media play a decisive role. Arthur Miller said at the PEN Congress at Bled (Yugoslavia, 1966): 'A technological society cannot exist without mass education and the same basic phenomenon is taking place everywhere, wherever the machine is prevailing, without regard to the political system—the masses have become the consumers of cultural benefits. . . . In short, I believe that literature will soon become public property instead of being reserved for a comparatively small number of people. . . . But it may be even harder to become reconciled with the fact that ideas, to which we always thought people would be insusceptible, have suddenly become common property.'

Through the mediation of mass media culture becomes international, cosmopolitan and it surpasses local, regional boundaries.

With economic, cultural, political and technological advancement the contemporary world has achieved a high degree of mutual connexion and dependence, so that each new social or technological phenomenon that is at all significant outgrows the local scope and achieves a universal echo. The position or change in this position in one part of the world influences the position in other parts of our planet. This process of mutual influences and intermixture has been especially promoted in the last twenty-five years. With the help of space satellites mass communication is opening new, unforeseen perspectives to such a process.[1] It will be more and more difficult to limit culture only to certain societies, countries, regions, and the hermetic societies will find it more and more difficult to preserve their seclusion.

Mass media can perform an extremely significant role as an instrument of communication in world-wide conditions, as an instrument of communication among nations and continents, in short, among people. Thus they can help in creating an atmosphere of active coexistence and contribute an important part to the strengthening of peace, thus enabling progress in the world as well. It would not be wise, however, to close one's eyes to the other alternative, namely that mass communication media also act dysfunctionally by opening up just the

1. See the Report of the Unesco Meeting of Experts on the Use of Space Communication by the Mass Media, Paris, 6–10, December 1965.

opposite processes, the processes of disintegration in the contemporary society which serve the narrow interests of separate groups or countries.

'The meeting of cultures is the fate of our time.'[1] Under the pressure of socio-economic development, cultures that exist wide apart get closer and closer. From a cultural point of view the present world is very picturesque, although development is pressing the world to integration and homogeneity. Each nation has its characteristics in its cultural development and its special national culture which is the collection of historical traditions, a network of institutions, achievements in sciences, arts, philosophy, ways of behaviour, customs, attitudes, beliefs and values which are characteristic of each society. In the process of joining two or more cultures—where not only cultural contacts should be considered but also all the complexity of socio-economic bases and infrastructures—in the process of the so-called acculturation, mass media play a significant role as vehicle and catalyst at the same time.

Taken on the whole, cultures change slowly and gradually. The main factors which take part in the process of cultural exchange are economic set-up, social structure, geographic position, the degree of development in means of communication, frequency and intensity of intercultural communication, and, simultaneously, the growth of mass media as multiplicators of ideas and points of view.

The paradox of our time lies undoubtedly in the fact that the world has become small and accessible from the technological point of view, but it appears big and full of problems from economic, social and cultural aspects, because the present-day international world community is characterized by socio-economic differences, by its division into rich and poor, into 'haves' and 'have-nots'.

The gap between the developed and developing world is, objectively, the main paradox of the contemporary world. Historical necessity dictates to the developing countries an accelerated socio-economic development, but at the same time more and more obvious are the general tendencies in the development of the world to a closer interdependence of nations and to the integration of the whole of mankind in a universal human community. Mass media can be of a great help for the progress of the developing countries, especially if their action is synchronized with the component parts of social development, and if cultural values and population structure and spheres in which they are active are taken into account.

In the process of development the functions of communication do not change much; only the quantity of communication in a developing country is primarily changed. At the time of the Industrial Revolution machines multiplied human energy, and today, communication equipment at the time of 'the revolution of communication', the twentieth-century phenomenon, multiplies man's messages.[2]

The quantitative increase of messages creates favourable general conditions for national development; it makes scientific achievements easily accessible; it increases the extent of cultural exchange; it heightens the general level of aspirations. The increased flow of information creates fruitful ground for the growth of intercultural communication.

The quantitative increase of messages is not, of course, enough for increased national development. Mass media serve development as agents of cultural exchange. Thus they help the society in its transition from underdevelopment to a more developed stage, from the old traditional frameworks to a new social relationship. Contemporary mass communication media stimulate the process of cultural exchange.

It can then be concluded, from this supposition, that the stage of development of mass

1. Bergstasser in *Kulturen im Unbruch.* p. 28, Freiburg-im-Breisgau, 1962.
2. Wilbur Schram, *Mass Media and National Development*, Chap. I, p. 39, Stanford, Stanford University Press, 1964.

media depends upon the stage of social development, that less developed societies as a rule have also a correspondingly insufficiently developed system of communication. Because of this fact, mass media in the developing countries do not give such results as they could have given, if they had been correspondingly developed and fully used. It is obvious that in such conditions rights to culture cannot be fully expressed in these countries.

Contacts between societies are the factor that contributes most in the process of intercultural communication. But in the majority of cases equal communication among different cultures or societies is not involved, but a more developed civilization—mainly European and North American—breaks through. Modern mass media intrude from the industrially developed world into the developing countries. On the one hand, they stimulate the integration of insufficiently developed societies in these countries, on the other, they endanger the further existence of characteristic elements of these original cultures.

'The problem of cultural agreements is especially acute, not particularly when small countries are involved, ... but the problem is whether big countries esteem the unique cultural values which their small friends have', said Mr. Malcolm S. Adiseshiah, Deputy Director-General of Unesco, in one of his speeches.[1] The danger does not come from mass media themselves but it also appears in the manner of application and in the character of mass communication which accompanies other international, economic and political relations. Mass media are only the agents of the process of cultural exchange; but this can have its positive as well as its negative aims, functions, effects and consequences.

The process of communication among developed and developing countries is still mainly a one-way stream, thus unequal and inadequate. Therefore, there arises more and more frequently the tendency in the developing countries to maintain a certain distance in their relations with more developed countries and societies. As a young, growing economy tries to protect itself against the intrusion of highly industrialized countries with the help of protective measures, similarly the fragile structure of native, autochthonous, traditional culture wishes to protect itself against the massive intrusion of foreign examples, models and products of a social-cultural nature. As Schiller[2] asserts, the demand of developing countries for relative isolation is a means and an aim for the creation of native progress and international solidarity; hence the wish of many developing countries to establish such a policy of active coexistence which would allow the inner processes in different countries to mature. But the delicate problem of when and how to make the border between keeping a relatively profitable distance and between harmful seclusion, is left open.

The United Nations and other international organizations, especially Unesco, can play a significant role in the beneficial, positive direction of mass communication media by stimulating the progress of underdeveloped countries. The General Assembly of the United Nations presented a demand for 'a programme of concrete action for the introduction of print, radio, television and films into the developing countries'. In December 1962 this question was separately discussed and the significance of mass media for the development of insufficiently developed countries was confirmed. Unesco prepared special measures for establishing the degree of development of mass communication media. The direct aim of the developing countries should be ten copies of daily newspapers, five radios, two seats in cinemas and two television sets for each 100 inhabitants. Nearly two-thirds of the world population still do not achieve this minimum presented by Unesco. Taking the present

1. Speech given at the University of Belgrade, November 1967.
2. Herbert Schiller, *National Development Requires some Social Distance*, AIERI, Hercegnovi, Yugoslavia, 1966.

degree of the growth of mass media into account (from 1950 to 1962) the above-mentioned Unesco minimum would be achieved like this:

Ten copies of daily newspapers for each 100 inhabitants, in Asia in the year 1992, in Africa only in 2035;

Five wireless sets for each 100 inhabitants, in Asia in 1970, in Africa in 1968;

Two seats in cinemas for each 100 inhabitants, in Asia in 1981, in Africa in 2042.[1]

All this proves the great task which lies before the less developed countries but also the responsibility of developed countries in surmounting the hundreds of years of time lag, to assure the basic conditions for the assertion of rights to culture.

Mass media have great possibilites in the positive process of cultural exchange: they can forward fundamental, valuable ideas and achievements from the treasury of human thought, they help to form taste and awaken needs for a certain quality in culture, they help in the mutual acquaintance of different cultures, sub-cultures and intercultures.

Some of the mass media which are not linked with the spoken or written word, but which are based on the visual element, can especially work in a more direct and thus a more efficient way. This refers particularly to such media as TV or cinema and also to some branches of art, as music, dancing and plastic art.

In establishing rights to culture and in the process of cultural exchange the language differences often present a great obstacle. This is true of the intermediation of cultural achievements not only among different nations, but in some cases also of separate, multi-lingual societies and countries. Cultural achievements of small nations that do not speak one of the major languages are mostly handicapped. An excellent writer of a small nation can be much less known and read than an average writer of a big nation. To a certain degree, this handicap can be observed with mass media, too.

The contradiction which is known in nearly all societies and which has not been abolished yet by the modern world is such that those who need cultural development most have no appropriate possibilites for it. Mass media develop more quickly in the town than in the country. The shortage of media is to be found just there where they are most needed. Thus rights to culture are not equally reflected even within particular countries or societies. A similar case is to be found in social spheres: the need for books and reading is least developed just in the cases of those people who need a book most. Mass media make this contradiction less sharp, but they have not been able to solve it.

One of the basic conditions for the realization of rights to culture is the general level of education of people. Education is one of those factors which helps most in the transformation of an individual or society. 'Media of information must play a significant role in education ... new techniques of communication should help especially in the advancement of the process of education.'[2] Mass media can help in education directly as well as indirectly; they can substitute school activities or enrich them, they can take over the role of the teacher especially in such cases when there is a shortage of teachers, they can help in the education of adults, in complementary education, in the fight against illiteracy, etc.

Just to add a few words about the contradiction between national identity and universal integration. This contradiction cannot be solved only in the field of mass media, although it is strongly present here. In the present age of prevailing tendencies towards and processes of integration in the world, the nation outgrows itself in economic, political, and especially in cultural aspects. The nation becomes a composite part of the world market, of the political and cultural community, although numerous characteristics of individual nations remain

1. Wilbur Schramm, op. cit., Chap. III, p. 113.
2. United Nations General Assembly, December 1962.

untouched. In the interests of the true integration of humanity there should neither be complete preservation of national originality nor absolute destruction of nationality. But it would be wise to find a form in the integration of humanity which would preserve the sovereignty of a nation and at the same time make possible the approaches to the single cosmopolitan community. But this is only possible through the free, equal development of all nations and by overcoming all the differences which separate the world today. Man should be protected so that he may keep his right to his own national cultural values, and at the same time he should be able to have the right to enjoy all valuable cultural achievements and benefits of the present world.

Discussion

T. Martelanc   The subject I was invited to write about is so vast that I got the impression that any kind of working paper dealing with mass media would be insufficient, inadequate and superficial. I tried to overcome this difficulty by making the paper longer. I will not go into my paper in detail, but I would just like to add a few characteristics of the problems posed from the aspects of mass media. When dealing with mass media it is impossible to avoid touching on other related problems of the agenda. Because of this, I would like to limit the framework of the subject, not its scope. First of all, what I am stating in my paper is that the role and activity of mass communication media depends upon the social set up.

Mass communication media do not operate in a social vacuum but in the centre of a system of social interaction and among social elements that are linked together and which depend upon each other mutually. Thus, mass communication media are shaped by the society and vice versa. It is true that mass media may influence certain cultural parts of a whole society, but nevertheless they are an integral part of the whole social and economic set-up. This means that they are also influenced by the benefits or drawbacks of the society in which they function. However, I think we should admit that they have, by their wide diffusion of culture, created a new social dimension of culture. In this connexion I wish to state that the expression 'mass' when speaking of mass media is not identical with the same expression usually used in connexion with culture. It is true that culture achieves, thanks to mass media, mass, or universal character, but mass media diffuse products of élite as well as of mass culture, and for this reason it is only possibile in my opinion to speak of culture, one culture, and of the role which mass media have in spreading it. For instance, I have seen on shelves paper-backs which print Shakespeare, or Goethe, or even some ancient Greek philosophers, alongside horror stories or pornographic stuff. On the radio or television you can listen to Mozart, Bach, Haydn, or to some of the worst rubbish of so-called 'entertainment' music. So, as I said before, culture can be from the point of view of quality either good or

65

bad. And this is defined by the way in which it is being transmitted, or by whom it is being received. The element of 'mass'—mass diffusion, mass distribution, mass transmission— is actually basic for the implementation of rights to culture. There is another aspect of the limitations of mass media, which is that basically the same laws apply to mass communication as those which apply to a dialect or to personal communication; this is that mass communication does not exist by itself or as a precondition of a social life. On the contrary, it is the social life which enables this communication. Communication is one of the basic characteristics of man as a social being, and in the process of communication the individual asserts himself as a social being. Therefore, communication is a social process. There is also a kind of mutual influence in formulating values and attitudes. It is true that mass communication cannot replace completely direct interpersonal communication, but it is also true that it is not entirely different from it. It is also quite true that each type of communication differs greatly in quantity, but in content there is actually no basic difference between mass communication and traditional ways of communication. Bearing this in mind, I tried to define the role of mass media as a means of political and economic propaganda, as a vehicle of cultural exchange and, above all, as an indispensable means for the socialization of man. As such, the mass media are becoming a real social power; they are conquering the whole world, and they are sowing the seeds of social change. Mass communications media not only feed man's leisure time, they not only mediate entertainment information, but they also creatively influence man's thinking, his attitude to life and his behaviour. But just because we recognize the enormous (but not omnipotent, as some sociologists claim) action and potential powers of mass media, we must at the same time stress the responsibility pertaining to the management and activity of mass media. This is something about which we have already talked and I agree that we should also have the right to control the creators—not the individual creators, but those who create culture values and culture images, those who give us the programmes through theatre, television and so on, because the misuse of these media, considering their over-all expansion and great potential powers, could be extremely dangerous. Mass media can play a very important role of communication in world-wide conditions. They can contribute, in no small degree, towards world peace, as well as towards helping progress in the world. However, we should not close our eyes to the other alternative, namely that mass communication media can also act dysfunctionally and can operate just the opposite process, the process of disintegration in a contemporary society, of serving merely the narrow interests of separate groups of some countries. When analysing the role of mass media a famous author used a formula which has since become classical: if you want to analyse the role of mass media, you must answer four questions: who says it, what does it say, to whom is it said and with what effect? All four are rather important, especially the first one in my opinion. Who says the things to mass media? I was especially interested in what has been said here on the role of mass media in the context of the present world divided into developed and developing countries. It is quite true that we have a one-way pipeline that the process of communication between developed and developing countries is still mainly one-way, and because of that is unequal and inadequate. We know, as a matter of fact, that five main news agencies are really shaping public opinion in the world today, and they belong to four States of the world. There are about forty sovereign States in the developing world which have no news agencies of their own, and which are dependent on the sources of these main agencies. The same thing goes for television programmes. The United States is the greatest distributor and exporter. In Mexico, for instance, 98 per cent of all important TV programmes come from the United States, in the Philippines all foreign programmes come from American television companies. The United States television company ABC has got a programme network embracing all the continents. CBC makes the programmes for 76 countries. NBC supplies material to 303 stations in 81 different countries outside of the United States. This shows the tremendous one-way flow which we were discussing this morning, and certainly such a one-sided pipeline also creates a one-sided picture, which leads to one-sided values and one-sided images. Audiences get programmes which do not reflect their way of life or which are meant for audiences with a higher standard of life and a corresponding culture. They are being fed with something which does not correspond to the needs of developing countries. This is one of the causes for frustration among the developing countries, because these programmes create certain unrealistic needs among the audiences in developing countries. (I should add, here, that the same thing is also happening in the developed countries; after all the type of human beings personified in films by Sophia Loren or Elizabeth Taylor, are not very common even in the United States.) It is also true that audiences in a developing country, because of that, may know much more about the lives of people in a developed country, thousands of miles away, than they do about the people of another developing country which may be next door, or even about their own country.

At one point in my paper, I introduced a rather curious thought expressed by an American journalist, Herbert Schiller. He said that in the developing countries there is a growing tendency to maintain a certain distance towards the more developed countries. He even said that as a developed country tries to protect its economy by filtering incoming foreign products through customs barriers, so traditional culture is trying to protect its native, autochthonous pattern in the face of this mass intrusion of foreign cultural values from a developed world. Herbert Schiller has noticed that developing countries are demanding relative isolation with a view to creating national progress and international solidarity. He believes that this is the reason why we encounter a desire on the part of developing countries to elaborate a policy of active coexistence which would enable the inner processes of various countries to mature. This, of course, leads to a delicate problem: where to draw the line between a profitable distance and a too secluded isolation. In my paper, I have tried to illustrate, using some data, how wide the gap is between the developing and the developed countries, between north and south with regard to mass media. I go into some of the possibilities of mass media and some of the obstacles, but do not underline the advantages. Finally, in my paper I pointed out a contradiction which is not only found on the international level but within certain societies themselves, namely that those who need cultural development most have no appropriate means of obtaining it. This goes for the development on different levels of mass media in the towns and in the country. There is a shortage of media to be found just where they are most needed. The right to culture is not equal even between different social spheres of the same country. For instance, the need for books and reading is least developed in those very cases where people need them most. This brings us to the problem of free choice, or as I would prefer it to be called, the range of choice.

R. Thapar   It seems to me that all these discussions boil down to one basic point: the power behind it. If you go deeper into the problem there is the question of diffusion, of dissemination. This is, in fact, one of the vital fields.

There is an extremely important point which we should take up in our report, the question of finding some form of ideal control of mass media. We have to find an institutional answer to this problem, because of the other question which has been raised: who does the selecting? This is very important. Who decides who is to say what?

F. Debesa   I do not think you can make a culture develop by imposing extraneous elements on it; I think you can only develop a culture by taking very seriously into account the mentality of those people and the past of those people to whom a culture belongs. In my paper I underline three aspects of extraneous mass media which I consider have an important influence on the majorities of the population. First, the ever growing withdrawal of the regional cultural element. This is a fact, it is happening. Second, the mistaken indoctrination of youth of the underprivileged sections of society. This is related mostly to illiterates or almost illiterate people, who receive their first portion of culture through these mass media, and it is a culture from outside which looks very fascinating and glamorous to them, therefore they try to imitate it in a childlike way. The problem is that this sort of development, if you can call it so, is not taking into account the mentality of the people who are receiving it. Therefore it is not organic. As a result of this, we reach the third point which is that societies in these developing countries are being remodelled by extraneous values which bring with them a desire for wealth, power, refrigerators, cars, etc., and this creates what I call 'de faux besoins', for populations which have other much more urgent needs.

G. Lamming   The paradox that is to be found in certain poor societies is that, for reasons which have nothing to do with authentic communication, they have imposed upon themselves, or have had imposed upon them, some of the most sophisticated media of diffusion that the modern world knows. At the same time, we are informed by their governments, as well as by the people who set up these various installations, that they have neither the technical, nor the financial, resources for making the medium function as it should. The first, and essential, role of mass media in any form, whether it be radio, television or the press of a specific community, is to return that community to itself; in other words, it should let that community see and hear what it does. This, it seems to me, is its first priority. However, many of these poor countries cannot, in fact, return the community to itself since they are not in a position to make their own programmes about their own reality. The mistake made by poor countries, because they are poor, is to send would-be technicians for training abroad. Is it not possible to have technicians trained in their own countries? They should be encouraged to use their own society as the actual raw material of their work.

Another suggestion I have to make concerns writers. I have some notes here about the situation of writers who migrate from their areas. These writers have been responsible for authentic literature of their area, literature which is written in another society and published in another society. That is fine, but because of the cost of books, that literature becomes almost utterly unavailable for the people whose lives have been the very fuel of that literature. How can this situation be corrected? Is it possible for organizations to help in some way, perhaps by bringing out selectively in inexpensive paper-backs novels of writers from particularly impoverished countries, so that they may be made available to two-thirds of the literate community. My own books sell for thirty-five shillings. This can be the weekly wage of a domestic in Jamaica.

These are my two suggestions. The first is, in a sense, the most urgent, because it is through this form of mass communication that you involve at the same time the largest number of the audience which is already potentially committed to literacy.

R. Thapar   I would like to add to this very valid point you have made. We know, from our side of the world, that even though we have the facility to make films which interpret our life, these films are not acceptable to the television circuits of the world. The unions of technicians will not accept the films made in India because they violate union rights in

England and in America. Second, we cannot trust their interpretation. We shall be sent an impartial observer, and the impartial observer arrives with his ready-made frame to present our reality in a most distorted form to his audience. I would like to link the two-way communication with your first point. There I think we should take a very categorical position. If man is to understand man, as Professor N'Daw said earlier, as part of his cultural interchange and contact, the understanding between our territories must be through interpreters drawn from those territories, not from these so-called impartial observers.

F. Jeanson I would like to say that I consider this question of television of tremendous importance and I am rather concerned at the way what is said about it invariably reflects a certain pattern of thought which consists in wanting to train those engaged in television and trying to arrange that the State shall take over television, which, most of the time, would be highly unlikely to produce the desired results. It seems to me that this urge to bring pressure to bear on those engaged in television should be placed in dialectical relationship with the urge to provide the television public with enlightened information. Generally speaking, the same is true of culture: culture is a matter for the public concerned; it is not primarily a matter for the State, and no State should be expected to assume the sole responsibility of dealing with it. The public concerned has always, in my view, to face up to political power of some kind, and what I was referring to just now by the term 'cultural action' (since more detailed information has been requested on the content of such action) is, in the case of television, making televiewers gradually more politically-minded, and this can only be brought about by various means which I would term 'professional'. At the moment, this is our only means of defence, or rather, offence—for that is, after all, a degree better than defence. I mean by this that the opportunity exists of bringing groups of televiewers to follow programmes on their little screen together and to start criticizing such programmes. This procedure offers, I think, great possibilities and would fairly soon be widely copied. It is true, of course, that we are in a paradoxical situation in which we have to deal with mass media while using methods that are not at all mass methods. However, a great part of our effort must be directed towards this goal: making it possible for men to receive what they do receive without being reconditioned, processed by it, and so, by degrees, managing to bring pressure upon those in charge of programmes.

Science and culture

by Nicholas C. Otieno

Science and culture is a topic so vast in scope, content, interpretation and definition that it would be impossible to give it adequate treatment by an individual in a paper as short as this one. People differ and experts will argue *ad infinitum* on whatever definitions might be brought forth for these two important aspects of human life. I will here attempt to give general definitions of the two terms, see where they dovetail and where they deviate from one another and then, finally, try to sketch the interplay of science and culture in the life of man.

Part of the problem which hinders agreement in definition is that all educational traditions have been based on the idea that there is always a cleavage between natural science and culture.[1] It should be noted, however, that science, by the use of the inductive method whereby generalizations are derived from particular observations followed by an interpretation of empirical rules so obtained in terms of unifying theories, basically tries to arrive at truth about nature.[2] It is, in other words, a discipline about the physical world obtained through scientific inquiry which has a metaphysical aspect where a belief exists that there is order in nature.

One further definitional and interpretative difficulty arises due to a confusion between science and the application of its results which fall under the general term 'technology'. The latter would be viewed as a body of knowledge concerned with the application of science to industry and production[3] whereby industry bases itself on specialized technical knowledge which relies on science, so that finally the end of the application of science is the control of the behaviour of matter so that man can manipulate nature for the material welfare of man with far-reaching effects on his cultural orientation. Bernard Shaw once said: 'Science is always wrong—it never solves a problem without creating ten more.' Whereas the first part of Shaw's statement could be rejected outright, there is some truth in the second part when we consider the effects which scientific appliances have exerted on mankind's cultural heritage.

Culture, on the other hand, would imply two qualities which Matthew Arnold described as sweetness and light, the latter looked upon as 'mental illumination' which comes from the acquisition of knowledge; the former viewed as 'sweetness' which implies humility, tolerance, sense of brotherhood and other allied humanistic values.[4]

One would go further and suggest that whereas science would be looked upon as curiosity about life, art as wonder of life, philosophy as an attitude towards life, and religion as a reverence for life, culture should be viewed as embracing and involving all these major facets of human life.[5] Culture is the never-ending curiosity towards the physical, the psychological and the spiritual—the unceasing wonder and reverence towards the ultimate facts of life.

From the above definitions, it would appear evident that the present situation in which

1. P. Jordan, *Science and the Course of Human History*, New Haven, Yale University Press, 1955, 139 p.
2. E. F. Caldin, *The Powers and Limits of Science*, London, Chapman Hill, 1949, 196 p.
3. R. J. Olembo, *East African Journal*, 5, 1968, p. 13–20.
4. T. M. Advani, *Cultural Forum*, 5, 1962.
5. R. Aiyar, *Cultural Forum*, 5, 1962.

science remains isolated from a traditional literary culture is anomalous and cannot last.[1] It is further argued that no culture can stand apart indefinitely from the dominating practical ideas of the time without degenerating into pedantic futility.[1] And although we have intimated earlier that science should be considered as part and parcel of our cultural heritage, it is now dominating our civilization with such far-reaching theoretical and practical ideas to such an extent that any consideration of culture must take it seriously. We do not mean that culture should be assimilated as such, since this would mean vast modifications in the structure of science itself; but science should be widened. If it were, it could be extended to social problems so as to become assimilated within general culture. Bernal stated, 'The world picture presented by science, which, though continually changing, grows with each change more definite and complete, is bound to become, in the new age, the *background of every form of culture*.'[1]

Science has bearing on the good life (cultural aspects) in that it can help to stimulate the intellect, discipline the will and help to form a full mind and a firm character. All these, we contend, it can only do if it takes its proper place in a liberal outlook, in an 'open culture'.[2]

The place of science in society, however, is too often considered in the narrow setting of economic welfare alone, so that the potential contribution of science to culture is underestimated. Science should be viewed in the wider setting of its relation to thought, art, literature, religion and practical needs. This view was endorsed by the meeting of OECD ministers, who went further and recognized the role science should play in public policies of governments. They saw a double aspect of science which they termed 'policy in science' and 'science in policy', in which they saw a technical, economic, and political aspect of science which touched on, among other matters, the cultural well-being of countries. The culturalists, on their part, must examine individual ideas, organizational biases, institutional attitudes, operational realities and the necessary compromises out of which national decisions emerge and how science will go about contributing to the achievement of national cultural goals.

Today, we need a scientist who is conversant with philosophy, history, art and literature; whose studies would be fruitful and beneficial to society. In the same way, as an example, a truly modern historian should be required to be conversant with natural science, since the history of scientific inquiry belongs to the essential substance of history.[3] It should be noted that some of the most fruitful germs of scientific activity were derived from Greek culture.

From the foregoing outline it would appear that science and culture are both an integral part of human life which we can only separate to the total demise of man as a whole. Results of the application of science are with us and I believe these will more and more contribute towards the realization of Unesco's Constitution which seeks to give 'fresh impulse to the spread of culture, assuring the conservation and the protection of the world's inheritance of books, works of art and monuments of history and science'. Examples which may illustrate the role of science in the preservation of man's cultural achievements are many, but a few will be mentioned. The application of the machine to remove the great temples of the Nile to safer places where they will be available for posterity shows breathtaking achievements of science in the field of cultural preservation. Werner describes the useful work being done in the United Kingdom for the conservation of antiquities by the use of products from high-

1. J. D. Bernal. *The Social Function of Science*. London. Lowe & Drydone. 1943. 422 p.
2. E. F. Caldin. op. cit.
3. P. Jordan. op. cit.

polymer chemistry through a wide range of new synthetic materials which have been discovered.[1] These are used as adhesives and consolidants for the repair of fragile antiquities and as waxes for the restoration of objects damaged by water. Harald envisages techniques and potentialities of employing electronic computers in musicological research.[2] Here, musical data would be stored in computers which would later lead to the use of electronic systems in musical analysis.

The artist will be, and is, profoundly influenced by the microscopic designs revealed through crystallography and the marvellous symmetries revealed through the study of microscopic plant and animal parts. The architect is now beginning to employ the 'mathematical great circle' to construct gigantic geodesic domes which will enable humanity to pursue his activities in cities where there will be no microclimatic changes to interfere with his activities. The revelation of new forms in other planets by use of satellites should stimulate the poet to cease being earthbound by producing verses which will, in turn, enrich humanity's culture immensely.

The use of the telephone, the radio, the cinema and the television annuls space and time to such an extent that hardly any cultural entity has remained untouched.[3] These have now provided cultural avenues through which cultures should meaningfully evolve.[4] We may, in fact, start to talk about a world culture which would be a fusion between religion, spirituality, and the world of science and technology. One recalls the saying of the late Mahatma Gandhi: 'The windows of our house should be open to all the cultural winds of the world.' Hence it will be well-nigh impossible to safeguard traditional and minority cultures from absorbing cultural influences from without. The best we can hope for, and we must strike out boldly in this line, is the welding of cultures into an unarticulated unit while making sure that many values inherent in individual cultures are not destroyed. Herein lies our dilemma.

But, within specified geographical units, we might achieve cultural unity and integration if we reject individual autonomy, at the same time accepting unity in diversity. Through scientific appliances, individuals have, to a lesser or greater degree, access to other cultures; and he would be a naïve person who would be willing to predict the multi-purpose channels through which these interactions will go. This is where governments—through a central co-ordinating body—should institute studies that will endeavour to resolve all the many variables so as to give us a meaningful whole.

While the present trend of having access to other cultures through discoveries of science, i.e. cinema, radio, etc., is a good thing up to a point, in that it enlarges the experience of an individual by imaginative participation in other kinds of lives, we are at a cross-road in that it is not at all healthy when this kind of wish-fulfilment occupies much thought— and when there is such a great contrast between the reality and the dream.[5]

In conclusion, it has to be accepted that technical knowledge has increased and is increasing at such a pace that our cultural heritage might be caught napping. Science is on the march, but it must be integrated with culture—as handmaidens walking together towards the realization of man's greatest dreams: peace and happiness.

1. A. E. A. Werner, Scientific Conservation of Antiquities, *Endeavour*, 27 (100), 1968, p. 23–7.
2. H. Harald, *Elektronische Datenverarbeitung in der Musikwissenschaft*, Gustav Bosse Verlag, 1967, 248 p.
3. P. Jordan, op. cit.
4. R. Aiyar, op. cit.
5. J. A. V. Butler, *Science and Human Life: Success and Limitations*, London, 1957, Pergamon Press, 162 p.

From nation State
to international community

The right to culture and the
Universal Declaration of Human Rights

by B. Boutros-Ghali

By the right of an individual to culture, it is to be understood that every man has the right of access to knowledge, to the arts and literature of all peoples, to take part in scientific advancement and to enjoy its benefits, to make his contribution towards the enrichment of cultural life.

This definition, inspired by Article 27 of the Universal Declaration of Human Rights of 11 December 1948 and by Article 4 of the Declaration of the Principles of International Cultural Co-operation of 4 November 1966, presupposes, in fact, two postulates.

It assumes firstly that the individual has attained a 'standard of living adequate for the health and well-being of himself and of his family, including food, clothing, housing and medical care...' (Article 25 of the Universal Declaration of Human Rights). For, if the individual has not reached this standard because he is undernourished or even starving, because he has no decent lodging or lacks the possibility of receiving the most elementary medical attention, it is evident that he will have neither the desire nor the possibility of taking part in the cultural life of his community and there can be no question of his enjoying the arts and literature, still less of participating in scientific advancement.

In other words, the concept of natural rights is, at the outset, without value for more than half of mankind. A minimum of material well-being is necessary if the very notion of culture is to have the least significance.

Secondly, the mere existence of cultural rights supposes that the right to education, as set forth in Article 26 of the Universal Declaration of Human Rights, has first found a practical application. Indeed there is no right to culture without a minimum of education. The person who can neither read nor write and who has not received the most elementary instruction is impervious to any true culture. And, a large part of humanity remains illiterate.

Which being said, some sociologists, taking the word 'culture' in a broader sense, maintain

73

that 'mass culture' can, owing to new methods of collective information, reach the individual without his having first acquired a minimum of education.

Despite an element of truth in this view, it remains that an illiterate has much less chance of being able to take part in the cultural life of his community and that the claim of cultural rights is not in his case matched by any tangible reality.

Thus it seems that the content of cultural rights will vary according to whether these two prerequisites have or have not been realized. The two prerequisites, 'right to an adequate standard of living' and 'right to education' have never yet found a true application over a large part of the planet.

If the Washington-Moscow axis is defined in terms of power and wealth, the Tangier-Djakarta axis is expressed in terms of existence and underdevelopment, and the right to culture cannot have, in these two worlds, the same content.

To give a practical example, it is necessary to distinguish what are these cultural rights in two entirely different socio-economic contexts: a consumer society and a society in course of development.

Cultural rights in the consumer society

The problems raised by inclusion of the right to culture among human rights, in a consumer society, were considered at length in the working paper. All the same it is desirable to emphasize certain aspects which must be considered in order to determine the content of these cultural rights.

1. The practical realization of cultural rights must allow a larger participation of man in the communal life to make up for the mechanization and anonymity of industrial society. One might speak of arriving at a shared management of industrial society through the influence of culture.
2. Implementation of cultural rights must enable man to free himself from the grip of publicity by giving him the means to contest and to discriminate between the different sources of information.
3. A consequence of effective cultural rights is to make known to the consumer society the existence of other societies and other cultures. The question is not so much to develop peaceful and friendly relations between peoples as to bring them to a better understanding of their interdependence. Culture, as an instrument of international solidarity, may perhaps preserve our planet from a class war on a State scale, where proletarian nations would face peoples in possession.
4. The wider spread of culture will also allow the consumer society to pay more heed to the dangers of its power and to the vulnerability of any civilization.

In short, full development of the cultural rights of a consumer society must lead it to restrain its desire for power and to understand better the determination to exist of the developing societies.

Cultural rights in a developing society

It would be a mistake, when defining the concept of cultural rights in a developing society, to follow the same lines as those applying to a consumer society. Cultural rights in a developing society have characteristics of their own.

1. The first of these is that the content of cultural rights will be closely linked with the political right of self-determination. This quest for an indigenous culture as a means of liberation and rebirth was vigorously expressed by Leopold Senghor, President of the Republic of Senegal, in a speech addressed to the Addis Ababa Conference of May 1963:

74

'That which unites us lies further back than history—it has its roots in prehistory. It belongs to geography, to ethnics, and, above all, to culture. It is older than Christianity and Islam, it is older than all colonization. It is that cultural community which I call Africanism. I would define it as the totality of African values of civilization.'

2. Cultural rights are also closely attached to the concept of rehabilitation. A new meaning has to be found for national dignity; traditional culture must reveal new values belonging to a community long colonized. The Emperor of Ethiopia explained this idea in these words:

'Some thousands of years ago, flourishing civilizations existed on this continent. These were in no way inferior to those which existed in other continents at that time. Africans were politically free and economically independent. They had their own social structure and their cultures were truly indigenous...'

This same idea was echoed by Sekou Toure, President of the Republic of Guinea, when he said:

'Not one of our nations taken separately would validly represent Africa nor fully rehabilitate its peoples. African civilization, African culture, African humanism, in a word the contribution of Africa to the life of mankind requires from all African peoples their conscious presence and their united action in the work of constructing universas happiness...'

3. The concept of cultural rights in underdeveloped areas is closely associated with the idea of development, much more than with the idea of leisure. This means that the right to culture is still identified, to some extent, with the right to education. A practical education which aims at helping the individual to master the poverty which is his lot, before troubling itself with his culture or that of the community. Leopold Senghor developed this idea thus:

'Awareness of our cultural community, of our Africanism is a prerequisite of all progress towards unity... I do not deny it, we have in common also our situation as underdeveloped countries.... But it is precisely in order to escape from this material and technical situation, that we must summon up spiritual energy...'

Self-determination, rehabilitation, development, all are motive forces that will dominate and fashion the content of cultural rights in underdeveloped areas.

Is this to say that cultural rights must be divided into two different categories?

This division is, of course, temporary, and the more the gap between rich and poor nations closes, the nearer we shall come to a universal concept of cultural rights.

It would therefore be a great mistake if in order to preserve the myth of universality, we were to frame a general concept of cultural rights out of keeping with the present international combination of circumstances.

From nation State to international community

by Yehudi A. Cohen

There are two problems in connexion with a conceptualization of cultural and human rights. What do we mean by 'culture' in terms of human rights? Where do these rights reside, i.e. who has them?

The evolution of human social organization has currently reached the point at which all people are—or soon will be—members of nations. The social organization of a nation is qualitatively different from that of a stateless society, in which local community autonomy is one of the most prominent features of socio-political relations. Increasingly we are finding that the concept of culture as developed by anthropologists in their studies of stateless societies has many gaps and weaknesses when we try to apply it to modern nation States. Increasingly, in almost all societies, the community—to say nothing of the individual—lacks the power to control the institutions that regulate and determine its existence. Local life is based on modern techniques, equipment, products, controls, goals, and values that originate in distant places; that is, almost every community is constantly and increasingly dependent on material and cultural imports. More and more, these imports originate in other countries in addition to the country of the community itself.

Thus, it is necessary to change the conceptualization of culture. While it may be good for the tourist industry, the notion of culture which rests on exotic customs, dress, colour and foods is rapidly becoming irrelevant. Instead, it is necessary to conceptualize culture in terms of the socio-political realities of nation States. One way of doing this is to conceive of a nation in terms of relations among groups within a politically centralized society; these groups not only include the local community, class and ethnic groups (and castes, where they exist), political parties, religious and non-religious groups and the like, but also the bureaucracies of the State itself. The relations among these groups refer, *inter alia*, to co-operation in the realization of common goals, and to rivalries and conflicts in acquiring power, prestige, material possessions, and control over sources of energy and means of production.

While current daily headlines seem to belie this, we are moving quite rapidly toward the development of a world community; the United Nations is the present political representation of this community. One of the principal features in the histories of nations has been the loss of autonomy by the local comunity in the service of increasing centralization of socio-political and economic control. Another important feature in this aspect of cultural evolution has the attempt by almost every State to replace cultural heterogeneity by national cultural homogeneity. An integral part of this process is the replacement of local symbols and loyalties by those that are uniform throughout the society. Specifically, this refers to the replacement of local by national traditions, the displacement of local educational systems by centralized systems, and the establishment of nation-wide media of communication in order, in part, to facilitate the dissemination of national symbol systems. In other words, the State is the respecter of no community or other localized nexus of tradition, custom and belief. While we may deplore this as private individuals, to expect States to act otherwise is to expect that they do not behave as States.

This is often confused by many observers as connoting the development of a world-wide cultural uniformity and standardization. However, if we look at the total record of cultural evolution, it is an inescapable conclusion that cultural variety and heterogeneity have steadily increased with every major advance in socio-technological strategies of adaptation. One of the principal reasons for this is that every such advance has made it possible for members of the species to inhabit and exploit the potentials of a greater variety of habitats. Man's current attempts to explore, exploit and, ultimately, inhabit extraterrestrial habitats are inseparable from the current trends toward the creation of a world-wide and politically centralized community. Treaties governing space explorations, the spread of nuclear-energy applications, WHO and Unesco activities and the like are inexorable parts of this process.

Cultural variety, then, especially among nations (as well as within nations) rests in large part on their strategies of adaptation in seeking to master more and more different habitats. Now, there can be no question that the development of a world-wide community and political system is going to entail commensurate adoptions of cultural patterns and limitations of national rights. At the same time, however, varieties in strategies of socio-technological adaptation will assure more cultural variety among nations than cultural uniformity. While there is no doubt that the world is daily becoming increasingly industrialized, this should not be taken to mean that all societies will perform the same activities. Some, especially the larger nations with great natural resources—but not exclusively these—will be the major producers of consumer products. Others, especially—but not exclusively—the small nations with limited natural resources will probably concentrate on what are generally referred to as science-based industries. Other nations of different sizes and endowment will tend to develop in still other directions. It is the right to develop along such lines that can be considered among the most important in the modern world, and which must be guaranteed and protected within this emerging world-wide community; correspondingly, it is just such development along lines that are compatible with local national resources, potentials and limitations which should be encouraged in developing patterns of international co-operation and exchange.

These rights therefore are the rights of nations (to this should be added: to the extent that the problem can be conceptualized in our present stage of knowledge and intellectual development). Culture is a characteristic of groups, not of individuals. Hence, when we speak of cultural rights—which I take to mean the right to maintain the integrity of a culture—we are speaking of group rights, the privilege that a group enjoys *vis-à-vis* others to maintain its style and strategy of living. In stateless societies, people's principal identifications—in terms of loyalties and allegiances, obligations, expectations of help in times of need—were with their local kin groups and communities. One of the goals of centralized States is to deflect these identifications from local nexuses to the nation as a whole. By a similar token, one of the goals of a world-wide community and political system will be to claim identifications and allegiances that, presently, are national.

However, one of the things that is currently observable in many major nations is that governments are having considerable difficulty in maintaining a balance between loyalty to the State and allegiances to ethnic groups, among others. The modern world is still too young to provide the historical perspective from which to learn how these problems will be resolved. It is still too early to tell whether the counterposition of, for example, national and ethnic loyalties is a transitional phenomenon or a permanent feature of the national cultural scene. This needs to be investigated; since these problems are often most acute in those societies in which the social sciences are most highly developed, it is to be hoped that the opportunity will not be lost.

77

One way or the other, such investigations and analyses will be able to provide some guidelines and hints for the future and will make it possible to engage in realistic and intelligent long-range planning. For example, are local loyalties—to ethnic groups—such an inexorable part of the human condition that they will continue to be part of the scene, whether as loyalties to ethnic groups or nations, when a world-wide community and political system becomes even more of a reality than can be imagined today?

If it emerges that ethnic or other local loyalties are to continue as important aspects of the national cultural scene, nations are going to have to be encouraged to facilitate the development of educational systems, for example, that will exist in tandem with the States' educational systems for those who wish it. But this must be done on a basis of rational planning, not on an *ad hoc* basis. Perhaps more important, an emerging world community can also be expected to develop an educational system that is appropriate to its organization and interests. In this case, too, a balance is going to have to be sought between its orientations in the educational sphere and those of the individual nations. This is essentially similar to the problem that has been faced since Sumerian times, of working out a balance between the local community and the State with respect to economic and legal relations and regulation.

But regardless of the sphere of activity in question—law, education, economic regulation, health and welfare and the like—it is not sufficient to say *ex cathedra* that this group or the other has an inalienable set of rights *vis-à-vis* all others. These are statements of faith that have little to do with the realities of the socio-political and economic conditions under which people live. What must, instead, be considered are the interests and imperatives of the most inclusive groups in which people live—today, nations; in the future, an international community—in relation to the needs, resources, potentials and limitations of their components. These considerations refer to balances, not to compromises. It has generally been characteristic of politically constituted groups to recognize the interests of their components in terms of conflict and dispute over rights that they consider to be limited. But this need not always be the case; can the leaders of nations, for example, be convinced of this? In the matter of education, for instance, would it not be possible to establish a world-wide programme in which all the nations of the world teach their youngsters about the international character of technological advances, about the contributions made to technological developments by people of different countries. That is only one example, and it can be multiplied many times. But what is to the point is that most contemporary education is, in one way or another, highly chauvinistic and nationalistic. Would an international effort to make education more international in character be an infringement of national, or of any other, rights?

I have not said anything until now about the rights of the individual, and I have deliberately left this for last. As with the rights of nations and other groups, I do not think that it is possible to make any statements *ex cathedra* about these, although the Universal Declaration of Human Rights should arouse little controversy as far as it goes. Since human life is inseparable from society and culture, it is axiomatic that the rights—together with the obligations and liabilities—of the individual stem from the organization of the group or groups in which he lives.

Communities enjoy personal freedom, dignity, rights to all sources of knowledge and information, interaction with representatives of other cultures, and the like, when their political rulers are secure. Generally, policies of mass slaughter, terror and degradation of the individual have been characteristic of nations in their early stages of development, when national ruling groups are insecure and uncertain of the loyalty and obedience of their communities. When these ruling groups become more and more certain of themselves and of their subjects, that is, when their political and economic control becomes increasingly effective and free of organized challenge, they tend to relax many of their restrictive controls over the individual and give him more personal freedom, afford him a greater measure of personal dignity and other rights. The status of artists, poets and others is usually a good index of this. Policies that strengthen national régimes—rather than weaken them—are the instruments which ultimately assure the securing of individual rights.

I would like to conclude by adding one qualification to this. While it is often fashionable among many people, including social scientists, to yearn for the days of yore when it was the small autonomous community that was the locus of most social life—and at the same time to deplore the tendencies toward greater centralization of national controls—let us also remember that it is the small and tightly knit or inbred community which is the source of the most restrictive and rigid controls over the individual. It is the small and highly personalized community which is the most effective inducer of stultifying conformity, of restrictions on social and intellectual manoeuvrability, of reductions in alternatives in life style. It has been in nations in which the conflict between State and local community has been strongest that the State has resorted to mass slaughter and terror in order to demonstrate its power and authority. Generally, when centralized States have not been challenged by the local community or other localized nexus of authority, they have not had to resort to the degradation of the individual as a means to legitimacy.

One of the lessons that can be drawn from this aspect of history is that the individual enjoys the greatest amount of personal freedom when the ultimate sources of authority and control are furthest removed from him, as in nation States. Thus, the task facing the species is not to try to resurrect the local community, but rather to strengthen nations and—ultimately—the political institutionalization of an international community.

Discussion

Y. Cohen   I would just like to make a few comments about some of the basic premises that underlie my thinking in this paper. When we start talking about the rights people have, one of the things which we have to keep foremost in our thinking is the fact that people are no longer deriving their rights (political, economic, religious, educational, etc.) from their local communities. They are, instead, deriving them from their nations. And the nation is not just an overblown community. A State, a national State, is a vastly different phenomenon from a community: it is not quantitatively different, but qualitatively different from it. In many countries all over the world discussions take place currently in which people talk about going back to the warmth, the intimacy, of the small community, while, at the same time, the central State is becoming more and more dominant, controlling more and more of literally every aspect of their lives. The State is not only here, but it is here to stay. Whatever rights, whatever security, whatever obligations, whatever privileges, whatever liabilities people have are no longer derived from the local community, but rather from the State. To a large extent, it is understandable that intellectuals, liberals, radicals, etc., find it very difficult to accept the legitimacy of State powers, the State authority, the State might. Generally it takes a great deal of time for people to accept new forms of authority. However, one of the things which we have to start talking about is the fact that the State *is* the dominant institution, or that State institutions are the dominant institutions in every nation. Even these are really a redundancy; in time to come it will be an international organization which will increasingly dominate a world community. If you look at the whole evolution of human social organization, you will find that it has moved steadily, at clearly understandable rates, slowly at first but more and more rapidly as we approach today, from the local band to the lineage, from the lineage to the community, from the community to the region, from the region to the nation, and from the nation to what we are all moving to right now, namely the beginnings of a world government of a world community, with the United Nations as the current political representation of this world community. People resist this, and if you go back and look at the record of human cultural and social evolution, you will find that people have resisted the development of clan authority over lineage authority, the development of regional authority over local clan authority, and so on, and that they have fought the development of nations. Similarly, because basically the species has not changed that much over a few million years, our people are resisting or fighting the development of an international community and international government.

The other assumption that I used, upon which I relied heavily in my paper, and which has been taken up by several people here, is that people do not derive their rights from the very fact that they are human. There are no inalienable individual human rights; people have always derived their rights from their groups. If you change the nature of the group in which people live, you almost automatically change the nature of their rights. Today, people derive their rights from nations; they derive their rights by virtue of the fact that they happen to be members of this or that nation. We can anticipate that once we get the real beginnings of a world community and a world government we are going to find ourselves having to discuss what kind of rights we should have. I do not know what form these rights will take, but we shall find that we are talking about new kinds of rights that we have never talked about, either before or now. I think that there are many advantages to be gained by living in States rather than in small, autonomous, tightly knit and tightly controlled, communities. Whatever the manner in which we define rights and freedom we find that they are always at their greatest in very strong and very secure centralized State systems. However, in this connexion, we have to bear in mind the fact that the vested interests of a State are those of uniformity in economic behaviour, uniformity in political behaviour, uniformity of the symbol system, uniformity, or near uniformity, of religion, ideology and intellectual content. This is in competition with the aims of local traditional cultures, and, of course, it leads to problems. What do people do once they have lost the advantages that exist in the small community?—for I don't wish to leave the impression that I think that the small community has no advantages; it has many. But, now that it is on the decline throughout the world, one of the questions we have to ask is: what are people going to substitute for it? What new relationships are they going to develop with themselves, with their habitat, with their society, with their friends, with their kinsmen or with their neighbours? And what are the maximal advantages to be derived from living in a State society and, often, from living in an international society? What can people be made aware of, and how can we point to the direction which this awareness might take?

E. Gellner   When listening to Dr. Cohen's account I immediately thought of Switzerland. This is a minor point, but it seems to me quite interesting to note that Dr. Cohen did not apply his own principle of the strong State which can afford to be liberal to a major generalization he made about the linguistic policy of a State, the tendency to homogenize. As he observed, the State requires a homogeneous symbol system so that everybody can understand the instructions. I think this is true. One of the main factors in modern nationalism is precisely this requirement in a developing society of being able to communicate, i.e. having one homogeneous language in terms of which the educational system and the mass media can function, in terms of which instructions can be written. However, Switzerland is a very interesting exception which troubles me in connexion with this theory. I have tried to explain this exception to the first principle by applying another principle to it, namely that when the socio-political structure is very strong it can then afford again to become linguistically pluralist. Obviously, when the level of literacy is high you can get round the language problem, although this is not possible if there are other tensions. The high level of literacy does not prevent some countries where there is linguistic diversity from being precarious. In these cases the reason why the State does not attack the linguistic diversity is not because it does not need to but because it does not dare to. However, that dealt with a minor point. The main point I wish to make about Dr. Cohen's speech is to express the feeling that the more or less general disagreement with his paper on the morals of politics level should not blind people to the sociological content of what he says. People are upset by what seems to be a kind of *étatisme*, rights emanating from the State rather than from the individual, and this may not be a justifiable reaction, although it is certainly a plausible one. The criticism I would make of his paper is that he said a great deal, and what he said was drawn on a large scale; his generalizations would need to be qualified in detail, and it is obvious that one could have a long discussion about the way in which, by implication, he dismisses the whole thesis about the centralized State being the great danger to liberty. However, there is obviously important truth in the point he makes about the individual liberty depending, on the whole, on a stable structure rather than on a precarious one. This has to be elaborated upon. It would be very dangerous, for instance, to interpret him, as I am sure he does not wish to be interpreted, as saying that a strong State structure is a sufficient condition for cultural and other liberties. It obviously is not. What he did not discuss was the other necessary condition of liberty, namely the theme of pluralist forces, of some kind of pluralism, of liberty as the result of plural forces within a society of which the State machine is one. It seems to me that a very important point is being made, namely that it is the stable structures rather than the precarious ones which can, on the whole, allow individuals to be free, leaving aside the sociological question as to whether the individual is only manufactured, culturally speaking, by the society, and leaving aside the moral question as to where his rights emanate from: whether they emanate from his ultimate individuality or from his membership of the community. It could be more useful, for the time being, to look at the sociological side of the question—the extent to which cultural liberty presupposes a stable and reasonably effective system. What is more, this question seems to me to be particularly relevant to the theme we have been discussing so far, namely, access to cultural fulfilment. At this point, I would like to make a remark about a kind of confusion which can arise over this opposition between élite and mass cultures. The danger lies again in interpreting it simply as a kind of opposition between two attitudes, between people who value the élite or its culture, and people who have a sensitivity to the value of popular culture. The discussion should not really be phrased in this way—the reality is the other way round. The concept of élite culture has to be used precisely by those with strong egalitarian and democratic values, who are really concerned with diffusing something which is lacking, i.e. with diffusing the educational and subsistence means, the whole apparatus which will provide people with what they are lacking. It is precisely the egalitarians among us, or the extent to which we are primarily concerned with diffusion and equality, who must operate with a notion of élite culture. The reason being that élite culture is not only a notion with value content; it ought to be called a selective concept which highlights certain scarce features. The diffusion of culture in this sense should precisely be seen against the background of something similar to Dr. Cohen's reasoning, i.e. that it is only done effectively by reasonably centralized political and educational systems. The point at which it cuts across the other notion of culture is that one of the fulfilments which is being promised to the recipients of this diffusion, but one only, is the pleasure and satisfaction of nationalized and cultural identification. The fact that a language or a culture exists with which a man can identify himself should be not merely something taught at school by a possibly alien, possibly contemptuous, teacher, but should be something which is taught to him in a more intimate way by the environment with which he associates; it should connect not only with his technical skills but also with his moral and social being in his other capacities. Until this is the case, he has a certain sense of deprivation. One of the cultural rights, or pleasures, is identification with a culture. This means that one is then using culture in the anthropologists' sense, as something very broad, rather unselective, something which is not in short supply, so that in a curious kind of way one has to use both concepts. Each one requires the other, but also, in many cases, they are in opposition for reasons for which Dr. Cohen supplied the main premise, namely that in order to develop this effective machine which can diffuse culture number 1, you probably have to destroy a certain amount, inevitably, of culture number 2, although, at the same time, some of it is also required.

T. Martelanc   Dr. Cohen's brilliant and logical explanation of this paper fascinated me, but, in another way, it also frustrated me. If one goes to the final consequences of what he says, then the best thing an individual can do if he wishes to enjoy fully the rights of culture is to fight for an autocratic State. However, this is absurd. I do not suppose that Dr. Cohen meant it that way, but this is what I thought of when listening to him. Sometimes, I think that we apply too rigid a framework to certain aspects, so that we end up by opposing them, whereas they, in fact, are connected. For instance, traditional culture and national culture may appear to be opposed, but it seems to me that national cultures derive their roots from traditional or local cultures. National culture may be culture on a higher level, but it is enriched by the local culture from which it has emerged. When listening to Dr. Cohen I felt that man was being treated as an object, not as a subject who should be taking an active part in all the processes of everyday life, including politics, culture and so on. The aim of culture should be to free man's personality, to enable him to be creative, to enable his personality to develop to its full dimensions in order that he may take an active part in everyday life; he should not just be the object of the policy of a State.

B. Breytenbach   Switzerland has already been mentioned as an exception to Dr. Cohen's thesis. What about the Republic of South Africa? In that State the majority of the people have few cultural or other rights, and yet it is a member of the United Nations and is considered a viable state internationally.

K. Aoyagi   Dr. Cohen said that people tend to shift from living in communities to living in States. This may imply that the State brings centralization or concentration, but I have not fully understood the motives which are responsible for this shifting.

G. Lamming   We have talked about various kinds of States and various kinds of cultures and the problems relating to them. We have also talked about the way in which we are going to conceive these things, and there has been a demonstration to the effect that one way is to conceive of a nation in terms of relations among groups within a politically centralized society. It keeps occurring to me that the content of this thing you call 'group' or 'State' is people, and it is a little difficult to conceive of people in any existential confrontation quite in that sense. It seems to me that attempts to plan what we might do always have to begin with some consideration about the quality of living. You may be able to work out what you regard as a perfectly harmonious relationship between groups, but it may be a harmony of relations that is built upon sterility, upon the uncreativity of living. A man exists. He is there. However, he is there not as the chair is there, not as the piano is there, but as a being who is there in a state of consciousness, a consciousness that is not only aware, and has to be aware, of what is outside of it, of its external reality, but a consciousness that is aware of itself, a consciousness that has the capacity of reflecting upon itself. Now, it is this discovery in a man, which I think is inherent in all men, it is this discovery of a reflective self-consciousness that is the having of what one would call freedom. It is the discovery of this reflective self-consciousness that makes a man condemned to freedom, whatever his culture or his ethnic background may be. And the moment a man is condemned to freedom it is extremely difficult to see him as a group. And whenever you are going to think of groups you have to think now of a law of requirement, of a law of necessity, which this reflective self-consciousness makes upon this man, thus bringing him into tension with whatever arrangements you have. This reflective self-consciousness, it seems to me, is the 'having' side: what you might call a directive from within—a directive for freedom. This is in a reciprocal relation with the second aspect of consciousness which one calls 'doing'. That is, whenever he perceives external reality, whenever he perceives the effect of external reality upon himself, his next move is always the move towards how he is going to adjust to it, how he is going to suffer it, how he is going to enjoy it or how he is going to transform it. He is then in a state of 'doing'; 'having' and 'doing' are reciprocal. This connexion between 'doing' and 'having' is the very reason for culture, for what we may call music or fiction or poetry and so on, because, in all of our experience, it seems that culture in the form of the arts provides us with examples of the reflective self-consciousness operating at the highest possible level of intensity, at a level of intensity that is not the common experience of day-to-day living among men, although, in fact, it is fuelled by the experience of day-to-day living, or what is, in an anthropological sense, a general cultural situation. This relation of 'having' to 'doing' is the way in which these two are worked out: in other words, it is how we fulfil the total conditions of 'being'. In a way it is synonymous with consciousness, but it is continually expanding. In this connexion, I was very interested in the remarks made this morning about creativity. It seems to me that creativity is the informing which is basic to all living, at whatever level of life this activity is going on. I find all discussion about groups fruitless unless it is informed about the quality of living of the people inside or outside the groups. However harmonious relations may be, they would be sterile if they were not informed by this quality of living which, ultimately, is defined not by a super-structure but by the content of the groups.

V. Mshvenieradze   I have some questions to ask concerning Dr. Cohen's paper. Dr. Cohen writes that contemporary education is highly chauvinistic and nationalistic. What does he mean by this? My second question is whether Dr. Cohen identifies nations with States; sometimes it is not clear. Then he says that local tradition is replaced by national tradition. What does he mean by national tradition? Does it contradict local tradition?

Y. Cohen   As you know, my paper was based on a set of assumptions, and, obviously, no one ever assumes that a set of assumptions will apply to all cases. In fact, I use assumptions as a point of departure and then try to see to which causes they will apply. I will come back to this problem when I talk about different kinds of States.

A general question that was raised by several of my colleagues here was the distinction between moral issues and methodological or scientific issues. On the one hand, I am tempted to say that, of course, there is no morality in what I am saying; I am simply trying to describe and to understand what *is*. That, of course, is not so much an ideal position as it is an amoral position, and one of the things that I think about personally very often, as I'm sure many social scientists do, is the role of the individual: what is the role of the individual scientist as a moral person in conducting his scientific work? There have been many times, in various societies where I have done field work, when I have been forced to restrain myself, almost physically, from saying to people in the midst of what they are doing: 'You cannot do this to human beings.' Now, to a large extent the activity of science, the performance of science, is an amoral act. That is, one simply tries to look at what is happening, to understand what is happening, to describe what is happening; and then, on the basis of this analysis, one tries to find out where one goes from there, to find out if anything can be done about it. If not, what do we want to do about it? And, most important, one then has to ask the further question (which many people often overlook): what are the consequences, all the consequences, of whatever it is one is trying to do? Another issue which was pointed out yesterday and which I think it is very important we should bear in mind, is that at the same time that we tend to glorify, long for, or espouse, the ideology of the local community, one of the indices of the success of many nation States is the extent to which more and more people are coming to expect more and more things from their central national government, rather than from local groups.

Another question raised is what are the necessary conditions for human liberty, individual liberty, or the rights of groups—the rights of cultures. I would suggest that this is something we know nothing, or almost nothing, about, and it is unfortunate that the words, or the concept of, personal freedom, personal dignity, group freedom or group rights almost never appear in social science writings. I think that this is one of the biggest problems confronting social science today. We do not know what the conditions are, because it goes without saying that whatever happens in the universe, be it physical, social, emotional or anything else, can only happen under certain conditions. I think that rather than attempt to find out what the proper conditions are for the achievement of individual liberty, dignity and so on, one of the first tasks facing us should be to make this a respectable question in the social sciences. Once it does become a respectable question I think we can start asking social scientists to look at this rather systematically, although it would have to be studied internationally and not by members of any particular society.

Now I shall try to address myself to a few of the specific questions that were raised. Let us talk about the question of rights: what are rights, where do rights reside? From the point of view of what we are talking about here, one of the things that we, in this meeting, can say is that the very fact that the United Nations adopted a Declaration of *Human* Rights was an achievement of profound implications in human history which has not been fully appreciated. For the first time, representatives of most of the groups—most of the national groups of the world, I should add—got together and said: 'There are certain rights that all people possess, regardless of which groups they belong to.' I think that this is one of the indices of what I talked about in my paper, namely of a coming world community. My reasons for thinking this are the following: it was a characteristic of many human societies, until relatively recently, to speak of their own groups as being 'the people', the implication being that members of other groups were not quite human, not quite 'people'. Take the Nazi mass slaughter: one of the first things the Nazis had to do was to declare all the people that they were slaughtering as 'non-humans'. First they deprived them of their citizenship, and citizenship is the social definition of being human in a particular group. What we are now saying in the Universal Declaration of Human Rights and in this meeting is the very embodiment of what Unesco is, i.e. that all people have rights by virtue of the fact that they are human. This is a brand new development in human history.

It has been stated that we are living in an industrialized world. I should like to suggest the hypothesis that industrialization, and everything that industrialization represents, is inseparable from political developments. Industrialization is not only an economic system, but it is an economic system which is stimulated, controlled, governed and channelled into particular directions by political processes. Where attempts are made to industrialize societies without effective centralized control the industrialization does not succeed. If we start bringing economic and political factors together, which is where I believe they belong, we shall understand a great deal more of what is going on in the world. Most of the investments that are being made today in many societies, with a view to industrializing them, are not only economic investments but political investments as well, in the sense that they are investments invited or controlled by political bodies. Therefore, and this is the relevance of the point, if we say that industrialization affects the ways in which people live, i.e. affects their style of living or their quality of living, then we also have to recognize that these things are affected by political decisions and are not only the outcome of machines, capital, rules which govern labour, and so on.

I would like to return to the point that I made earlier about the assumptions that I was using and the fact that they cannot be expected to apply to all cases. One of the advantages of starting out with a set of assumptions, generalizations or hypotheses, or whatever you may wish to call them, is that you can then see to which cases they *cannot* apply, so that the assumptions can then be modified, thrown out, if necessary, or tailored to meet individual cases. The question was raised: what about Switzerland? I do not know very much about the cultural situation in Switzerland, but I would put the following questions in connexion with that country: how much room for manoeuvrability does an ordinary individual have in a small Swiss community? How much room for manoeuvrability does he have intellectually? How much exposure does he have to ideas from other countries? How much freedom does he have to express ideas that are deviant from the ideas of the majority? What are the risks of ostracism, what are the risks of being shunned, what are the risks of losing a job, as a result of expressing opinions that are deviant? How much room for manoeuvrability is there for, say, physical movement in respect of finding employment or different styles of life? These are not rhetorical questions, they are very serious ones, and it is on just such data that some of our considerations have to rest. If the data show that

Switzerland, for example, is an exception to the case, I would say that we cannot dismiss an exception simply by saying: 'It is an exception; well, we still have the rule.' I think exceptions have to be explained, just as rules have to be explained. Perhaps there is something fundamentally wrong with my set of assumptions. If they cannot be borne out, then I would be the first to want to change them.

As for South Africa, again, without trying to squeeze the toothpaste back into the tube, and make the cases fit the generalization rather than the contrary, it is my impression from what I have read and heard about South Africa that it is not a very secure State; it is a State which considers itself rather weak.

Another question that was raised concerned the rates at which nations develop. There is no assumption (and I wish to make this quite clear) that by virtue of the fact that a nation State exists it will show the same characteristics as all others at the same rates. No two societies develop at the same rate; nor do all societies follow in precisely the same steps in their development. If this were the case, all we would have to do would be to study one society to find out about them all. One of the many reasons we study so many different societies is to learn at what rates different societies develop and, furthermore, to learn which aspects of culture change more quickly or more slowly in different societies.

The question was asked: what is the definition of national culture as against traditional culture? There are many aspects to a national culture as against a traditional culture. One of these is, of course, the over-all system of symbols to which people will respond. When you call for people's obedience or mobilization, whether it be intellectual or physical mobilization, to whose symbolic call will they rally? There you have a very clear-cut example of the difference between local and national tradition. Religion plays a very important part in the national symbol system. Another example, less symbolic, but equally important in the establishment of a national culture as against a local or traditional one, is the extent to which nationally defined labour policies of recruitment, of control or of distribution will override local and traditional labour policies. That is one of the characteristics of many nations, and increasingly so in the contemporary world. You hire and you fire people according to their abilities, as against the local tradition of a small group, where you hire and fire people in terms of their personal relationships—in terms of who they know, who their kinsmen are or who their sources of influence are. We tend to take this for granted, but we cannot overlook it. Very important in the establishment of national culture as against traditional culture is the establishment of a national currency, of a national system of weights and measures—the ability of a State to engage in treaties which bind all the members of the society.

This brings me to another question that was asked: what do I mean when I say that education is chauvinistic and nationalistic? I did not mean these terms pejoratively, although they are pejorative very often. What I do mean by them is that the avowed objects of every educational system, since the first establishment of a centralized school system in Sumer, has been to teach people national traditions; to teach them to give loyalty and allegiance to a national system. For example, whether a society teaches its national history from its own point of view (and I do not know of a single society that teaches history except from its own point of view), whether it has a national flag at the head of the class-room or a portrait of its culture hero, it is teaching something to its children because they are facing it all day, and they associate what they learn with that flag or with that portrait. This is an aspect of teaching people to be loyal to, and respond to, national symbols, so that when necessary the leaders of the country can invoke these symbols and count on the automatic response of people to behave in a particular way to the symbols. It is not true that *all* national cultures have their roots in traditional cultures. It is true in many societies, but it is not true in all. The United States, which is very rapidly developing a national culture, grew out of very little that was traditional. A very important question is, of course: How far back do traditional cultures go? What are the limits? The concept of a traditional culture can be one of the symbols in a national culture, where a ruler says: 'Look, we are trying to preserve your traditional culture!'—without saying how far back that traditional culture goes, nor to what it dates, nor how many people in the multinational society happen to represent that traditional culture.

I was asked how I defined a nation State. Here, I would say that all definitions are arbitrary. I defined the nation as the geographical or territorial representation of the group. I, personally, use the concept of State to refer to the controlling centralized bureaucracies which rule and set policy for the various aspects of life within that nation, all the way from a prime minister's, or a president's, office to the bureaucracy that sets policies for the collection of taxes, the State being the political bureaucratic representation of national unity, national solidarity.

We all work at different levels of abstraction. Whether we are artists, scientists, skilled machinists, etc., we think at different levels of abstraction. As I said earlier, I agree with what Mr. Lamming said about the importance of the individual, the quality of being human, the quality of experiencing the sense of being human, the experience of 'I am'. But one of the things that distinguishes among people from different intellectual backgrounds is the level of abstraction on which they are working. True, I accept the criticism of social scientists that we do lose sight of the individual because of the fact that the level of abstraction on which we work is the group. The rationalization, the justification of anthropologists for continuing to work at this level of abstraction is that it is the group that remains, whereas the individual passes. It is the group which is a corporate unit, but the individual has a finite existence. Similarly, one of the things that I think should be explored is the question of intensity of personal experience which is allowed in different groups: to what extent of intensity is the individual permitted to experience his own self; to what extent can an individual say: 'I am being myself'.

Towards a new value system

Two cultures?

by Giulio Carlo Argan

The Universal Declaration of Human Rights of 1948 recognizes the right to culture. The question is, to what culture? Obviously, the right to culture does not mean the right to participate in a particular culture, which is given and imposed as if it were the only valid culture; it is not, in other words, the right to receive a ready-made culture. It is the right to create culture, or the right which every social group (and, in certain cases, even every individual) is acknowledged to possess, namely the right to play an active part in the community, regardless of its (or his) cultural traditions, religious beliefs, scientific and technical knowledge, moral or political opinions.

Culture is not a heritage, an accumulation of received ideas, but the method adopted by each social group to organize its own experience by relating it to the experience of others. In other words, it is the ability to undergo and exert influences according to a critical process which makes it possible to establish values by the analysis and comparison of facts. There is thus no difference between the ideas of culture and acculturation—the latter is not the material transfer of cultural products from one group to another, or from a higher to a lower class, but the inner movement, the vital dynamism, the process by which culture is created. If culture is thought of as a network of interrelations, we must also discard the idea of progress as something which can be achieved independently of the historical development of a civilization. Technical progress can accelerate or retard the rate at which civilization evolves, but it cannot substitute its own regular and mechanical movement for historical development, which depends on the dialectical and sometimes dramatic solution of the contradictions which are opposed to the ever greater integration of the community and to its final unification. The march of culture does not exclude the danger of regression, i.e. the danger that the network of active relations may shrink instead of becoming progressively wider: fascism and Nazism show that cultural regression can easily be associated with a remarkable degree of technical progress.

89

There are processes of acculturation between groups and within groups. To understand them, we must give up any idea of a cultural hierarchy; just as in world politics, there are stronger countries and weaker countries, but each of them preserves (at least in principle) its own autonomy, so there are richer and poorer cultures, but each culture retains its value both intrinsically and as a necessary component of universal culture. Cultural relations are not one-way relations: the culture of the communities of the Third World does not mean the diffusion of European or American culture any more than mass culture means the diffusion of the culture of an élite.

It must, however, be admitted that the idea of a monocentric culture, with a periphery organized around a radiating nucleus, survives in practice although it is discredited in theory. Too many people still believe that true culture means Western culture, even if we are obliged to recognize that modern Western philosophy owes a number of its themes to Eastern thought, or that Negro art has influenced the art of modern Europe.

Nowadays it is believed that we have finally achieved, with our technical and scientific culture, a universal culture, based on objective truths and rational principles, liberated from all references to historical traditions and specific forms of speech, equally valid for the élite and for the masses, capable of being disseminated immediately and everywhere and of providing practical benefits for the material existence of the so-called underdeveloped peoples. This is but another illusion. We may pretend to forget that this brilliant civilizing action conceals the horrors of brutal exploitation and shameful racial prejudice; but we cannot possibly countenance the false hypothesis that technological culture, because of its scientific basis, is a culture that transcends history. On the contrary, we know very well that it is only the latest, and perhaps final, phase of a cultural phenomenon which, since the nineteenth century, has been closely linked with the intellectual, political and economic history of Europe and America. Instead of regarding it as a universal culture, we should see in it merely a generalized form of a typically monocentric Western culture; nor should we forget that its dissemination within the original social group is due to the mechanism of its technical processes and the consumption of its products, whereas its dissemination outside that group is due to the violence and inhuman oppression of the colonizers.

Considered from the historical standpoint, what is nowadays spoken of as the 'technological', 'consumer', or even 'affluent' society must be looked on as a regressive phase of Western culture. Although technology boasts of its scientific origins, the dissemination of industrial products does not entail the dissemination of the scientific knowledge implied in their production, and even less the dissemination of a scientific spirit or conscience. By their very nature, industrial products are able to be used without requiring any knowledge of the scientific laws on which they are based. By asking to be consumed as swiftly and as completely as possible, these products appeal, not to reason and to its ability to judge and choose according to criteria of value, but to the unconscious motivations which give rise to irrational needs and to the violent impulse to consume—that is, to appropriate and destroy—everything. Moreover, technology, even if we grant its scientific basis, diverts science from its original final end, which is knowledge, by subordinating research to the needs of the market and the laws of profit. It would be absurd to identify technology with science; by posing as the new, and only truly modern, culture, industrial technology degrades and discredits both science and its natural and traditional framework, which is that of humanistic culture.

Objectively speaking, humanistic culture (including science) now finds itself in an impasse. Overwhelmed by the prevailing technology, it is still working on ancient materials, with antiquated methods and inadequate equipment. Many of those who are working in the field of the human sciences refuse to enlarge its boundaries or modernize its methods: they stick to the old territories of philology, philosophy and history; they are simply not interested in cultural anthropology, ethnology, epistemology, sociology, psychology, etc.; organized research and team-work are anathema to them. For their part, the power groups that hold the purse-strings can see no point whatsoever in supplying humanistic culture with the resources it needs to bring its organization and methods up to date; they would like it to retain its status as an ancient culture which no longer exerts any influence on the masses. The same power groups declare that they wish to concentrate their efforts on scientific culture, but, in fact, they support research only in so far as it forbears from taking a definite direction and submits to the exigencies, plans and objectives of industrial technology. Universities are no longer asked to produce scholars and scientists, but managerial technicians; it is desired at all costs to prevent anyone who 'practises' research from asking himself questions about the ethical principle, intentionality and ultimate ends of science—in other words, questions concerning its history and the true reasons for its development. Science is aided on condition that it does not regard itself as 'humanistic'; science and humanism are even declared to be opposites, as if science had not been for centuries an essential component of the humanistic cultural system. It is precisely against this reduction of science to technology that students are in revolt; they are unwilling to do no more than practise science and demand responsibility for it; they are no longer prepared to act as the depositaries and manipulators of a body of knowledge whose prime motives and ultimate aims are carefully hidden from them.

The real opposition is not between a humanistic culture, assumed to be concerned with art, philosophy or literature, and a scientific culture, concerned with mathematics, physics, chemistry, etc., but between pure science and applied science raised to the status of a sovereign science—in other words, between a science in which the claims of conscience are paramount and a pragmatic science obedient to the dictates of a superior, political power. Technological culture, being in the service of a system of economic power, is a politicized culture; humanistic culture (including science) whose unifying structure is history, is a political culture, whose fundamental task is to politicize the world. The words 'political' and 'politicize' have no relation here with current ideologies or with the parties that represent them; ever since its birth, humanistic culture has been a political culture, for it has always linked up the various disciplines with a unitary system of human coexistence on earth. These words, however, are used polemically—against technologism, for whereas the aim of the latter is to depoliticize the masses by concealing from them the historical significance of their acts, modern humanism seeks to politicize them, that is, to see that their acts retain that historical significance. Moreover, since there has been talk of a missionary vocation, the most necessary and urgent function of a modern humanism (which perhaps does not yet exist, save in a few sectors, but which could exist) is precisely to oppose the tendency to technicize society by reducing it to a manipulated mass, devoid of any historical structure and any possibility of political organization. This 'mission' can and must be carried out, either by social groups, especially by those who have most recently entered or are seeking entry into the world political system, or by classes, particularly by classes which have most recently entered or are seeking entry into the present-day system of equilibrium of active forces. Lastly, the problem to which every effort must be devoted is one of structures: the structure of cultural influences and their means on the one hand, and the structure of mass culture and its means on the other.

The common roots of our alienation

by Romesh Thapar

When I study cultural rights as human rights, I naturally assess their validity from the viewpoint of what is known as the developing world, part independent, part subservient—a world inhabited by two-thirds of mankind. An assessment of this kind brings into focus the hard core of the problems which are crystallizing as mass media penetrate the farthest hamlet, as education awakens the mind of the illiterate, as science and technology erode traditional thought and activity, as nations become neighbours, as the world shrinks and begins—or, at least, the developed part of it—to dabble with the concept of an understructure which is universal to our civilization. I say 'dabble' because in the haste to usher in this new era, no note is taken of the critical gaps in our understanding of social processes.

The pace is being set by those who possess wealth and power, by those who are arrogant enough to believe that the culture they have spawned is the medicine for all. In every developing land the virus has been planted through those who imitate mechanically, through those who are easily persuaded, through money and pressure, through patronage and sponsorship, even through innocent activities like cultural tourism. Two-thirds of mankind are being made to conform to a pattern of life which feeds alienation and which, significantly, is being rejected even by the sons and daughters of the élites of the advanced countries.

This is important to the dialogue we are embarked upon. The growing alienation in the industrial and technological societies—a vital factor in the crises of cultures—is now sought to be transplanted. Our developing nations of Asia, Africa and Latin America, which receive this supposedly civilizing touch, are now discovering that it strikes a parallel and more dangerous alienation—an alienation which polarizes the élites from their own peoples. This cultural disintegration sharpens the divisions already existing in societies which have yet to resolve the problems of inequality.

The intensity of this alienation-cum-polarization in our part of the world is also fed by the revolt of youth throughout the world who reject the established norms and perspectives of man's effort to advance. Advance in the directions indicated is considered retrograde, conformist, inimical to freeing the spirit of man.

There is now a deep contradiction between the value systems of established societies and the human rights to which we aspire. It is an explosive situation. The anarchism, nihilism, frustration and anger inherent in this situation can only be tackled by an alternative value system which has been carefully worked out, justifiable in humanistic terms, capable of providing the answers to the challenges posed by our massive entry into the era of science and technology. We have failed to create this value system of our era.

An antiquated value system cannot provide the base for cultural rights as human rights at this critical juncture in the lives of two-thirds of mankind who, as a result of the population explosion, demographically, have become younger. The enlightened among them realize that imitation of the rich nations invites traumatic shocks which our complex societies are unable to cushion.

In other words, the developing nations must learn from the tribulations of the developed.

Cultural rights embrace the whole gamut of rights—economic, political, social. They cannot be studied in isolation. And the totality of rights becomes meaningless when the value system at the base is itself being made irrelevant. This is the core of the problem and cannot be overstressed.

Let me reduce this to everyday language, taking the developing world as an example. Conditions vary from country to country, variations caused by historical accident and the adoption of differing patterns of political organizations, but certain broad trends are common to all.

The limited availability of national resources, and the urgent need to invest massively in basic development, compels a desperate search for free foreign exchange. Every avenue is sought, even slavish 'image-building' as a precursor for such aid. It is a self-defeating process, for the prices of primary products supplied by the developing world are for ever declining whereas the cost of capital goods from the advanced regions is rising. Even aid is found by our peoples to be repaid many times over.

A pertinent example of the effort to neutralize this subtle exploitation of the poor nations by the rich is the active sponsorship of supposedly self-reliant activities like cultural tourism for free foreign exchange—today one of the largest industries in the world. Innocent enough, but, in fact, tourism easily becomes the grave-digger of the cultural rights of the developing countries. The tourist infrastructure of most of our countries is made to conform to the tastes and needs of the visitors from the developed world. The cultural content of tourism is replaced by a dreary, expensive cosmopolitan style which has nothing to do with the habits and lives of the people being visited. All over the developing world, we can see the emergence of facilities which thoughtlessly repeat the norms in the developed world—bars, belly dancers, casinos, etc.

This manifestation of so-called affluent culture, together with the active role played by mass media, makes a deep cultural invasion of the values of the urban élites in our countries and over a period of time isolates them from their own people. Tourism is seldom a unique human experience. Change, in the context of creative modernization, is being snuffed out. Human understanding is not keeping pace with the shrinkage of our world. Such trends are sharply underlined particularly in those countries seeking economic relief in military pacts which underwrite their defence budgets and open the way for so-called 'rest and relaxation' centres for foreign soldiery. A terrible degradation is involved in this operation. It strikes down cultural rights and makes a mockery of human rights.

The popular response to this type of influence takes on a nationalistic, authoritarian colouring. Exclusivity and chauvinism are paraded as answers and soon win popular support. Isolationism of this kind breeds new evils—political, social and cultural—which are a threat to understanding and peace among peoples. Our developing world swings between these extremes and for the moment we are unable to strike a balance. Writers, artists, publicists, academicians, intellectuals and sensitive men of all disciplines begin to trudge the road which leads to alienation. The 'brain-drain' from the poor nations to the rich is only a facet of the tragedy being enacted.

You may well argue that these are issues to be settled by the prevailing power in each country, but when we speak of cultural rights as human rights we should see the intregal connexions between the two and the totality of human experience at this moment in our affairs. Meeting here at the headquarters of Unesco, we have to analyse the reality and project perspectives which correct the aberrations which we are helping to intensify by our apathy, our conformism, our indulgence in a value system which is in the throes of deep crises. Even those who are the sponsors of this supposedly civilizing process can no longer shirk this responsibility.

Admittedly, the task of correction has to be undertaken by the developing world, but we expect Unesco to be an intelligent and unflinching ally through its activities in the related fields of education, science, culture and communication. A new value system must be enthroned in the minds of men if we cherish change which is creative in human terms, designed to liberate the spirit of man. I believe this task can no longer be neglected for fear of offending entrenched political and economic interests, official or non-official.

We are, indeed, at the cross-roads. Enough of stereotyped history which falsifies truth and presents a lop-sided picture of each people's contribution to the development of human knowledge. Enough of economic theory which is mechanically applied irrespective of varying conditions. Enough of imitative technology which is wasteful and geared only to a consumption-oriented society. Enough of the new intellectual and academic colonialism which willy-nilly shatters the dignity and pride of newly emerging peoples. If cultural rights are to become an integral part of human rights in developing countries, a fundamental change in attitudes will have to be initiated and sustained by Unesco.

Inevitably, the process of correction will be long and arduous. Unesco, through meetings such as these, will have to evolve a plan of action for the developing world. Such a plan will naturally embody a certain flexibility to meet the special needs of particular regions of the developing world. Elitist cultural postures, traditional and revivalist cultural assertions, the growth and relevance of mass culture, the processes and content of cultural modernization, the position of sub-cultures, and many related questions, will have to be re-studied, in the context of the alienation resulting from the revolution of science and technology if human rights are to be fortified and nurtured. This should become the immediate concern of Unesco, or else its programme will not serve the ends to which this Organization is dedicated.

Unesco cannot permit itself to become the protector of a meaningless and explosive *status quo*. It must become the instrument of enlightenment. It must sketch the new perspectives before man, and make these perspectives the guide-lines for all its activities. I am asking for a revolution in social thinking to match the revolution of science and technology. Such a 'confrontation'—if it can be so described—is inescapable, for although I speak of the developing world, the roots of our alienation are common.

On the notion of 'non-public'

by Francis Jeanson

A preliminary clarification of the term 'non-public', by recalling the circumstances in which I was first of all led to advocate its use, will at once make its meaning more readily apprehended.

I refer to a meeting where all the promoters of theatrical decentralization and its derivatives in the form of cultural action came together in France for the first time. Convened at Villeurbanne (in the City Theatre) on 21 May 1968, for one day only, this meeting was actually to last for three weeks, after having turned itself into a 'Permanent Committee of Directors of People's Theatres and Cultural Institutes (Maisons de la Culture)'.

Since nearly all these men were in the theatre business (accustomed to thinking in terms of performances, that is to say, concerning themselves with the size and quality of audiences), no doubt they were already more or less aware of the danger of paralysis threatening their very lives as creators, owing to the existence of a public on which they were becoming ever more and more dependent, after spending twenty years in the effort to reveal it to itself. But although most of them were, in fact, trying in various ways to burst the bonds in which their very success was progressively enclosing them, they had never yet really succeeded in penetrating beyond the social stratum to which the majority of their 'customers' belonged. Whatever was tried—lowering the prices of seats, improving publicity, or even resorting to certain promotion techniques designed to render the proposed performances more accessible—any increase in the number of theatre-goers never reached beyond the potential public level, that problematical public which has not so far materialized, but which enjoys the same objective conditions of access to 'culture' as the existing public.

What the May-June events rammed home to them, with unexpected violence, was that it was no longer a question of extending this public but of turning at long last deliberately, and without paying the slightest attention to box-office considerations, towards the non-public; or, in other words, those who do not yet participate either in fact or potentially. Henceforth, this meant adopting a much more radical approach designed not so much to increase the number of theatre-goers as to provide those hitherto excluded from traditional culture with the means of cultivating themselves, according to their individual needs and specific requirements. And—who knows?—Shakespeare might one day become accessible to all. But what was first of all wanted was that each of them should be given the opportunity of acceding to himself and participating in the life of the national community on the same footing as the minority of privileged persons who, at present, are the sole beneficiaries of the country's cultural heritage.

Thus the use of the term 'non-public' was immediately understood by these forty persons responsible for cultural action based on theatrical representation as expressing their resolve to direct their efforts, beyond any search for a potential 'public', towards all those men and women who, as citizens, must be able to undertake their duties progressively in the sphere of public affairs.

The 'non-public', on the scale of any given society, is composed, in the first place, of all such as do not at present enjoy the means of access to 'culture', understood as being the generality of intellectual and artistic perspectives that are open (in such-and-such a domain and in varying degres) to members of a certain élite, 'cultured' people.

Among the means that are lacking to these 'non-cultured' people, the most obvious lies at the level of basic education, either because they were unable to benefit from such education long enough, or because their living conditions were such as to prevent them from deriving any benefit therefrom.

This lack presupposes another, more fundamental, one resulting from the politico-economic structure of the society in question. Statistically, the 'non-cultured' class is identical with the 'non-citizen' class, that is, citizens who, while formally recognized as such, are none the less kept isolated from those sectors where the important decisions are taken.

Thus cultural deprivation is more or less coincident with economic deprivation: the people deprived of 'culture' are, on the whole, the same as the ones deprived of benefits. On the scale of world society, as in the case of most of the individual societies composing it, the gulf is growing wider and wider every day between these outcasts and those who retain —to however small an extent this may be—the possibility of identifying themselves with the ruling social strata. In this connexion, it is not enough to declare that the countries belonging to the Third World are 'developing' so as to put an end to their constantly increasing effective underdevelopment compared with the economic growth of the industrialized countries; just as it is not enough to observe the increased sales of refrigerators and television sets so as to deduce therefrom that a definite social integration of the workers in the 'developed' countries has taken place.

In addition to this 'non-public' which has been objectively defined, we should mention two types of 'non-public' which cannot be wholly defined without recourse to certain subjective criteria:
1. The type found in 'consumer' societies, which comprises all those persons whose social condition places them in the path of culture but who derive practically no benefit at all from their advantage, in so far as they allow themselves to be hoodwinked by the commercializing (and more or less official broadcasting) of an ersatz culture which encourages them to proceed along their self-chosen path of the facility.
2. The type, which has made its appearance quite recently, which is composed of youthful elements (students and secondary school pupils) whose intellectual training steers them towards the ranks of the ruling social strata, but who are becoming ever more inclined to refuse to become integrated culturally with a social system which they denounce as absurd.

The passivity of the former is due to existing structures and contributes to their maintenance; that of the latter is also due to these structures but tends, on the contrary, to destroy them. It is an attitude of denunciation, a refusal to admit that culture can in any sense be confounded with a certain type of consumer products: those, on the one hand, which are widely distributed and backed by enormous publicity, relying on a rapid turnover in fashions and age-groups, and those, on the other hand, which are reserved for the benefit of an élite varying in size but always strictly a minority and justifying its importance on the basis of a more or less unassailable prestige inherited from the past. In both cases, 'culture' regarded in this way is only a choice between different states of importance since it no longer seeks in any way to place its 'consumers' or 'beneficiaries' in contact with the actual reality of their daily life and the innumerable forces which condition it.

In these various aspects, the non-public constitutes a veritable challenge for whoever champions a living and active culture, a culture enabling mankind to move forward together, day by day, towards a more authentic form of humanity. And the only way of meeting this challenge is by making a bet in favour of promoting a cultural attitude which rejects this social deprivation—and the menace of death which it involves for the individual consciousness—without however pretending to ignore its politico-economic causes.

The attitude in question must therefore be directed towards individuals in so far as their alienation within the social structure—however objective its causes may be in the majority of cases—implies at the same time a minimum of consent and passivity on their part, thus making them to a certain extent accomplices in the type of situation thrust upon them.

Cultural action aims not at transforming the social system, but at offering men the possibility of adopting a progressively more conscious attitude towards it and of participating ever more closely in the major choices that determine the community's present and future existence. In thus renouncing any possible connexion with action of a political nature (in the generally accepted sense), it constitutes none the less an undertaking designed to free the individual consciousness from all mystification and feeling of alienation, offering it instead the means of becoming 'politicized', or, if you prefer it, civilized; of becoming more and more capable of accepting its responsibilities in the conduct of human affairs. In this sense, all genuine cultural action favours transforming non-democracy, or purely formal democracy, into a democracy that is more and more real.

Such an attitude implies a conception of cultural life that is upheld by the demand for a practical demonstration of it in world terms. It points to a culture in the process of becoming, as opposed to one that is stagnant, already there, ready-made, a sort of sacred heritage which it is only a matter of conserving and transmitting. It even rejects—or at any rate goes way beyond—the naïve idea of a more just, more 'egalitarian', division of the cultural heritage, so far as the non-public distinguishes itself precisely by its more or less marked indifference to 'cultural values', which do not seem to it to bear the slightest relation to its actual problems of existence.

But, all the same, it doesn't go so far as to condemn out of hand a cultural past on which it is itself dependent and whence it draws its deepest motivations. On the contrary, its aim is to arrange things in such a way that culture becomes today for everybody what culture was for a small number of privileged people at every stage of history where it succeeded in reinventing for the benefit of the living the legacy inherited from the dead; that is to say, each time it was able to assist in bringing about a deeper sense of reality and closer bonds of communication between men.

Every form of cultural action, in so far as it seeks to be polarized by the existence of the non-public, must endeavour to provide this non-public with both the means of contesting and participating at the same time. This two-way function is the only social function which is able to become truly mediatory, by choosing to operate in a positive manner with respect to the collectivity as a whole, without contributing at the same time towards the mystification of one section to the advantage of another section.

Since the essential characteristic of the non-public is its non-participation, its non-integration in those very activities which claim to determine the development of the collectivity and define therein those values alone that are worthy of acceptance, any movement undertaken in its direction must start from the principle that it is utterly ignorant of the substance and forms of the type of culture it actually stands in need of. Consequently, cultural action is inconceivable except in the form of a permanent investigation conducted among those concerned and with their effective collaboration. And because the means at its disposal do not admit of its being directed straight toward the non-public in the mass, its only chance of being effective consists in proceeding step by step, or in stages.

For there is an urgent need to bridge the gulf and establish progressively valid relations with outcasts from the official, the dominant culture, as also with those who, in increasing numbers, choose to turn themselves into outcasts (from a feeling of solidarity, or simply as a protest against the absurd social lie that is being lived). However, it is not enough to be keenly aware of an explosive situation like this in order to be able to find the right cure for it, even should this be at the cost of virtually discarding the culture in which one has oneself been brought up.

If the 'non-cultured' do not speak the same language as we do, it is not only because their intellectual baggage has been less developed than ours; it is also because their experience of the world is different from ours, and a certain type of culture results therefrom to which we have no direct access. But the most lucid men and women among them have already understood that social dialogue will remain a dead letter so long as the economic structures (both on a national and world scale) continue to divide mankind into two camps—workers and beneficiaries. It is for this reason that any contact with this non-public depends, in the great majority of cases, on an effective collaboration with the various organizations which form its permanent means of defence and its agents for collective advancement amid societies where the ruling social strata tend to pursue interests which are not its interests.

It is true, however, that any cultural action which confined itself to conducting a purely sociological type of investigation among the non-public would be doomed to failure. In the case of culture, people's real needs are not readily expressed in the form of conscious demands; they can only be progressively discovered at the cost of plunging into the unknown, in other words, by putting forward such-and-such a proposal knowing it in advance to be more or less off the point, but relying on it for that very reason to provoke reactions which will be the means of sparking off a genuine dialogue.

If it behoves the culturally privileged to make the greatest efforts in this direction, that is because their own existence can only have real meaning through their throwing themselves heart and soul in to this permanent task of social mediation. In fact, we shall only be able to call this world ours to the extent to which it really and truly becomes more and more that of all men, in which all men together will be capable of creating values mutually recognizable as such.

Today, the fate of humanity appears ever more and more dangerously at the mercy of social conflicts which tend to set men against each other. For this reason, all cultural action must henceforth be concerned with collaborating—in its own way and according to its own methods—in a sort of world mutual civic literacy campaign, in the success of which its organizers cannot fail to be as interested as those on whose behalf it is launched.

Discussion

A. N'Daw   Just now, someone used the metaphor of the pipeline, an extremely attractive one in itself, but which has bewitched us to the point where, if I am not mistaken, it has induced us to examine cultural problems in a one-sided way. I think that it is legitimate to present cultural problems in terms of reciprocity and equality between the productions of the developed and developing States. All the same, this is a one-sided aspect. I think ʒhat cultural problems are also matters of interest for the developed countries, or shall we say, the countries with a technological civilization. The question of culture has been raised also in Europe and also in America. I imagine that we can draw a distinction between the Europe which, thanks to its so-called technological civilization, has been able to export its culture and impose that culture or the products derived from it on other nations, and the Europe which, by a sort of boomerang effect, has had its spirit deeply corroded by the weight of that same technological civilization. This is so true that we ought to discuss it. A distinction must be drawn between cultural problems as they present themselves in the developed countries, where they arise despite the existence of a very strong technical and technological framework, and cultural problems as they present themselves in the developing countries. We have been told how Europe is in danger of being bored to death because it has lost that spirit which was, precisely, the motive force behind the development of those scientific activities which, to my mind, have degenerated into technology. We ought, therefore, to look into the cultural programme in the developed countries, discover why the people are dissatisfied with the affluent society. However, possibly the fact of posing the problem of culture in terms of opposition between the developed and developing countries would enlarge the scope of this notion of cultural rights. If the Declaration of 1948 omitted to mention cultural rights explicitly in connexion with the individual, the reason for this is perhaps that in the structural framework of the developed countries a certain accessibility to culture is taken for granted; that is to say that, apart from having his immediate biological needs attended to, man aspires to a life of the spirit and to what can form him into a responsible human being. The reason why the problem of cultural rights has only just lately arisen in Europe is because there is such an abundance there of material goods that greater masses of people can now satisfy all their basic living requirements, with the result that now they hanker after something different.

In the case of underdeveloped countries, the problem presents itself in two aspects: firstly, restoration; secondly, diffusion. There is, first, the claim to a culture of their own, owing to the fact that these countries were under foreign domination. Colonialism begins by destroying the personality, by taking away from peoples in subjection their historical drive and turning them into mere objects of history, instead of what they should be, subjects of history. Hence, colonial emancipation led these peoples to claim, in addition to their political and economic independence and (perhaps before this) their cultural independence, because that was the only way they could assert themselves, justify their rights as a nation, a community, responsible for its own existence. The claim to an indigenous culture, to recognition of its value and the right to its diffusion—all this is manifest in the writings of intellectuals from those countries. There must first be a restoration of the individual culture. In connexion with this, and turning back for a moment to the statement by Dr. Cohen, I think that he tends to confuse tradition and folk-lore. I believe that, over and beyond mere rituals, mere external forms of expression, what is really called tradition is a spirit, a spirit which can take on such-and-such a form. All that need be done is to allow these peoples to retain their natural dynamism. Tradition must be a source of inspiration. I think that everything that has been criticized as capable of holding us back, preventing us from entering the modern world is simply the by-product of, the fall-out from that tradition which, at its source, is a living movement. Culture is something to make us live, not something to make us fat. That is the essence of culture. I think that to try to preserve certain stereotyped forms of traditional culture is against the interests of our true culture. I maintain that all culture is a living thing, that cases of fall-out present themselves, and that there are, therefore, certain elements which, unable to adapt themselves to life, disappear of their own accord. Wherever you find the true spirit of traditional culture, I do not believe it can ever be in contradiction with modern culture. I am convinced that the absorption, integration or assimilation of modern techniques are essential conditions for enabling our indigenous cultures to recover their dynamic qualities and express themselves. I believe that the idea of cultural rights first appeared in the form of a claim by a certain group *vis-à-vis* another group. At the group-to-group level, I think that one can ascribe a definite meaning to the idea of cultural rights. It must be looked at from the individual level too. If you compare what takes place in Europe with what takes place in the developing countries, you find that in Europe culture is looked upon as a luxury; and yet the consciousness of cultural claims, of cultural needs has nowadays become so widespread that the satisfaction of such demands is now seen to be among the most crucial interests of that sector of the population which hitherto was solely concerned with earning a living. At the individual level, in Western countries, the consciousness and satisfaction of the need both to participate and to create come immediately after the satisfaction of the basic requirements of life. Among the peoples of the Third World, the need is essentially to restore the indigenous culture to its rightful place, breathe new life into it, so that its influence may be spread.

B. Boutros-Ghali   I should like to take up again an idea which has been put forward and which, as it has aroused special attention, constitutes an essential element in our discussion. This idea, to use the picturesque metaphor of the cultural pipeline connecting the developed part of the world with the developing part of it, is that this pipeline does not function properly. It transports cultural products from north to south, but does not transport similar products from south to north. This lack of communication, this inequality in the cultural movement is one of the main problems in connexion with cultural rights. Yesterday, we were given many examples of this, more particularly, as between the United States of America and the Caribbean countries, and as between the United States and Chile. American culture comes and imposes itself in the Caribbean, in Chile; but Caribbean or Chilean culture cannot penetrate the consumer society of America. I could give numerous examples drawn from that part of the world to which I belong. French, English and American culture impose themselves, pass through such a pipeline into the Arab world; whereas Arab culture, apart from the products of certain specialized institutes and certain specialists in Arab affairs, has no chance of penetrating the French, English and American consumer societies.

It seems to me that it is this inequality which should be recognized as the core of the problem. How is it that the culture of the rich countries, the consumer societies, manages to impose itself; manages even, to some extent, to place in jeopardy the culture that is sometimes referred to here as traditional culture? And why doesn't this traditional culture manage to penetrate the consumer societies? The initial answer might be that the cultural pipeline was built for the purpose of transporting the cultural products of the West, but not any other kind of products. It was the rich countries who built the pipeline and consequently it is they who run it, and they don't want the products of the poor countries to pass through it. Then, it may be answered in line with Dr. Cohen's thesis, that the cultural products of the Third World are inappropriate for export, which is why they fail in this respect. This deserves to be examined. How is it that, for example, American films please an Arab audience and that Arab films fail to please an American audience? Apart from the pipeline which doesn't function properly, it is possible that the cultural products of the Third World have not the same export potential behind them as the cultural products of the wealthier countries. So far, we have not considered this aspect of the problem; yet it is a factor we should take into account in seeking a solution to this inequality. So we come back to this question of inequality. Judging from what has been said, it is primarily due to the available means of transmission, what I call the pipeline. This pipeline functions only in one direction, because it is in the hands of the rich countries. Here, we must be practical. What exactly can be done to try to solve this basic inequality—an inequality due in the first place to the means (the pipeline which the Third World doesn't possess) and, secondly, to the fact that the cultural products of the Third World are, to use Dr. Cohen's expression, inappropriate, because they fail to be exported to and accepted by the public in the rich countries, with their consumer economies? Here, that mediator who has been referred to between author and non-public must be invented at the international level. We have got to find a mediator between the rich countries, the countries that control the pipeline, which enjoy an over-abundance, and which have too little difficulty in exporting their culture, and the poor countries, which indeed have a culture of their own, but are unable to export it. If, therefore, a mediator is needed between author and non-public (such as exists in certain countries), I consider that a non-public also exists on a world scale, and it is formed precisely by the peoples of the Third World. Such are the broad outlines of the problem: how to establish that minimum degree of equality which makes dialogue possible. Unless that minimum exists, dialogue will forever remain impossible.

It follows that what we are seeking is not perfect equality; that will never exist (moreover, if perfect equality existed, there would be no such thing as cultural integration: the latter can only be produced on the basis of a certain inequality); but just that minimum of equality which will make it possible for the pipeline to function in both directions. This brings us to a further aspect of the problem: not only do the pipelines not function, they attract away from the Third World the few cultural elements that exist there, whether it be in the teaching profession or in the sphere of the arts, thus bringing about the flight of the élites, the brain drain. That's the first problem. Then there's a second problem, of a practical order too: how can the Third World, in a practical manner, manage to break loose from the educational and communication systems that have been imposed on it, either directly through the colonial system, indirectly through a species of neo-colonialism, or again, as a result of inequality at the start? This is the situation we have to deal with: an overflow of cultural products of the rich countries, whereas the cultural products of the poor countries are unable even to find a local market. That is yet another difficulty.

To conclude, allow me to revert to the idea of the third party, the mediator. I don't know quite how we are going to invent this mediator. At one moment, the idea of an international institution crossed my mind. Whatever form this invention may take, it will have to be at the international level, so as to counteract the present inequality of communication in the pipeline. A double role would be assigned to this mediator: it would be responsible for transmitting, for endeavouring to attenuate the effects of the cultural products from the rich countries, and also for trying to make the rich countries aware of certain intrinsic qualities in the cultures of the developing countries.

Y. Cohen   One of the thoughts which has occurred to me often during this meeting is that we have been enclosed in this sound-proofed room without windows talking to each other, which means virtually, given the stratum of society from which we are drawn, that we are talking to ourselves in a circular fashion. What is going on here could be called a monologue rather than a dialogue. Are we not doing just exactly what has always been done by élites (and we are élites, whether we feel guilty about it or not, whether we are conscious of it or not, whether we like it or not), that is to say, deciding for the masses what is good for them and informing them of the decisions once they have been made? Could we not democratize this kind of discussion? Would it not be possible for conferences such as this one to be conducted out in the open, for this kind of a session to be held on a stage with an audience from a local society (and this would mean holding such meetings in many different countries), so that the people who work, who have jobs, who don't speak our language, can hear us and so that we can hear them? We could then get a dialogue going between us élites and the people out there about whom we are talking. Such meetings as I have suggested might get us away from the fact that it is the centres of power, the decision-making apparatus of modern nations which always control the media of communication. As a matter of fact, I think that this is one of the definitions of a politically constituted group—that it does control the media of communication. This happens in every type of society. Obviously, it would be impossible to broadcast the proceedings of such meetings to the world, but wouldn't it be possible to get outside the given institutional structure— almost like the people who are very often referred to, and dismissed as, the objects of 'brain drain', who have become international and who, to a large extent, are serving a very important function in the world today just because they are international. (In this con- nexion, we have not exploited these people; we have not used them, and they are very usable—in fact, they are among the people who have some of the most important things to say in the world today.) Instead of talking to each other, could we not go to the people and let them hear what we think? It would also give them a chance to react to us. That is where, I think, the important things lie—outside this room.

F. Jeanson   I have just been listening to a species of self-criticism. If it is not just a custo- mary rite in a meeting such as this, could we not perhaps make use of it in order to help us devise a new method of operating, complementary to existing methods, and which would be marked by an insistence upon continually closer relations with the populations con- cerned? To my mind, it is of capital importance that we should be able to penetrate these populations in depth—and the matter is urgent. I was asking myself yesterday whether we were really collectively aware of this urgency. I was rather surprised by a certain academic tone in our discussions and by the impression I got that each one seemed to think he had eternity before him. Actually, I think we have very little time indeed in which to give practical proof that we really are of some use, that we have an active part to play in present-day situations—situations which I, personally, regard as explosive, everywhere, both on a world scale and on that of each country. It is high time, I think, that a positive campaign were launched—a civic literacy campaign, shall we say—the aim of which would be to persuade men everywhere to regard themselves as beings responsible for the successive collectivities to which they belong, right up to that ultimate collectivity known as humanity and which,

102

as far as I know, has not yet been brought into being. I suggest that we ought to review our very methods of work. Personally, I am very happy to be among you, to observe that problems of this kind can, in fact, be discussed, which I regard as already an extraordinarily positive gain in itself. All the same, a meeting of this kind would have been more useful if, for instance, three people without any special qualifications of any kind, had come instead of me. It is time we got people to come who are not university products, who are quite unknown, and who dont't belong to any particular élite, and gave them the opportunity of discharging the most important responsibility of our time—that of mediator, go-between. So long as we fail to incorporate such go-betweens, we shall have accomplished nothing. I would have preferred, indeed, that my place had been taken by three young people (I say young people because I think that such persons are, in fact, the most free, most accessible, least hidebound) in situations such that they are in contact with the non-public.

We must ask ourselves if what Dr. Cohen has just suggested can be put into practice. An organization like Unesco, making the best use of the means actually at its disposal, ought to use them in such a way as to enable those concerned to exchange their points of view, and by those concerned I mean just anybody: just anybody, provided he or she is in a position in his or her own local surroundings to address other men or women living in the same locality. Generally speaking, I should like Unesco to use its means for intervening more and more directly in people's lives, undertaking action at the level of representative men and women, with or without any special claim to being 'important'. What matters is their ability to address other people, to see to it that an idea is definitely converted into something concrete.

Numerous countries have been referred to where the dissemination of documentation, information, etc., is inadequate. It appears that even where such exists, it remains to all intents and purposes inoperative, owing to the almost total lack of any real go-betweens among the population. Whether it is a book or magazine, television or any other mass communication medium, we are always paralysed by the fact that these media are invariably in the hands of people who take as little interest as possible in those matters which concern us. Might not the first necessary step (one with a chance of determining the practical use of everything to follow) be to manage to establish more or less everywhere active cells which would take charge of publications and put them into practice, in the same way that television clubs or associations can be organized where people watch the programme together and then criticize it with the idea of bringing about changes in its content? Every day we see more clearly that what hosts of young people are crying out for is a mission to give meaning to their lives; they want a cause; they are begging us in all kinds of ways to help them find one. I do not wish to imply by this that there are no longer any causes, any missions left in the world. The young are fully aware that causes exist throughou the world which deserve to be upheld; but they then come up against an obstacle—their own honesty: for it is not in Angola that they wish to be employed; it is here, at home. But here, at home, a whole host of problems exist side by side, none of which, however, is on such a scale as to convince them that by setting themselves to solve any or all of them they could give meaning to their lives in the midst of a consumer society characterized by absurdity and boredom. We have got to put youth at its ease, and the only way to do this so that they can confront problems going beyond the bounds of their own country is to demonstrate to them the essential interaction between their country and other countries, and, on the home front, between the social stratum to which they belong and the rest of society.

The youth of today ought to consider working in common with the youth of other countries; in the same way as they should consider working within their own country in common with young people whom they have never met because these happen to belong to a section of the population with which, even in a 'civilized' country, a certain fraction of that same population has practically never any contact. Would it not be possible for an important international organization like Unesco to examine the possibility of bringing together the youth of different countries in a closely-knit, organized fashion for the purpose of common action? Something after the style of an international public service, the lack of which makes itself felt more and more alarmingly every day, and which, in any case, is a necessity from the point of view of social order, for we are heading straight for the abyss. A huge chasm cuts right across the world, and a similar chasm is to be found in each country, particularly in the developed countries. The two are all the time aggravating each other, and unless we take care the situation will soon get out of hand.

Replying to another question, I would say that classical culture—the body of existing works and ideas going by that name—cannot possibly do anybody any harm; it doesn't do us any harm, apparently, and it cannot do any to those who do feel unconcerned with it and are totally ignorant of it, or are kept out of range of it. 'Comics' can certainly be classed as a form of culture, but I fail to see in what sense they are a more practical form of it, that is to say, offer people the chance of getting to know the world and supply them with the means of transforming it. On the contrary, I regard them as an escapist form of culture which, in the last resort, caps an absurd by another kind of absurdity, which is simply more amusing. It doesn't change anything, it doesn't contest existing reality in any way, it doesn't offer men the means of adopting a fresh, more conscious attitude towards that reality. 'Comics' are, in a way, a negative cultural expression. In my opinion, culture is all around us, at all times; it is there in a compartment of the Underground when two people pass each other, one of them going to take a seat and the other preparing to get off: their way of passing each other is all part and parcel of culture. The question is whether this culture is creative, inventive, or whether it is simply a composite of human relations that are in process of disintegrating, stagnating or falling asleep. My own view is that culture is really and truly a function of human relations, in the sense that men have to be continually reinventing them.

Statement on Cultural Rights
as Human Rights

PREAMBLE

This meeting was called to consider the relation of cultural rights to human rights. It was intended as an opportunity to examine the meaning of cultural rights as these affect the individual and to consider the responsibilities of individuals and Member States in ensuring these rights.

The following conclusions were reached by an international group composed of scientists, writers, critics and analysts:

1. The Universal Declaration of Human Rights, drawn up in 1948, has had a profound influence on our thinking about the rights of man. But the world has witnessed very radical changes during the last twenty years. The spirit of the Declaration may have survived these changes, but the revolution of science and technology as well as the political liberation of millions of men requires a new perspective and a more realistic application of skills and intentions to the urgent needs of mankind today.

2. Culture is a human experience which it is difficult to define, but we recognize it as the totality of ways by which men create designs for living. It is a process of communication between men; it is the essence of being human. Millions of men and women are dangerously deprived of the fruits of culture in the classical meaning of the word. It would be dangerous to support the view that these benefits are the prerogative of the few. This legacy cannot be organized and distributed by a national or universal élite. There must be a full recognition of the diversity of cultural values, artefacts and forms wherever these appear. The first task of life is to live and one of the principal functions of culture is to enable people to maintain and perpetuate life. Hence we assert that all people must have equal access to those instruments which make possible the physical perpetuation of life as a necessary precondition for all other enjoyments of life, including spiritual and material values and the products of creativity.

   The most important precondition of life is peace. One of the principal functions of cultural interaction is to eradicate wars from the life of societies.

3. Today we need a living culture which would enable man to master the reality around him. The widespread survival of poverty in a world possessing the means of affluence presents a tragic obstacle to fulfilment of human rights. This unequal distribution may, and often does, engender false values which further obstruct a full life, adding a moral insult to the injury of poverty. Affluence is not a standard by which men can judge exclusively their work and capacity as men. Culture is everything which enables man

to be operative and active in his world, and to use all forms of expression more and more freely to establish communication among men.

4. The uniformity which is imposed upon culture by the consumer society (by the term 'consumer society' we mean consumption at a level higher than is necessary and as an end in itself) and its impoverishment by the intensive advertising of false standards and values is sought to be justified as the logical outcome of the revolution in technology and industrialization. Socio-economic structures, within nations and those which link nations, strengthen this trend and heighten the threat to the development of living cultures. Positive and constructive answers to these questions can no longer be delayed.

5. We cannot underwrite a *status quo* which fails to grant these rights, and by its failure invites a violent response from those who are deprived. We require a revolution in social thinking and action in order to cope with the revolutionary challenge of science and technology. The rights to culture for the poor throughout the world must begin with their liberation from poverty, disease and illiteracy. Freely elected governments should be protected from the intervention of foreign countries through military, economic or political coercion.

6. One of the characteristics of our contemporary world is the domination of men by strong centralized nation States which have the power to increase cultural uniformity and homogeneity within their borders and outside. While such cultural uniformity and homogeneity is understandable from the point of view of the political and economic interests of the ruling groups of such societies, means have to be found to mobilize those cultural traditions the richness of which can provide people with a sense of belonging to coherent groups and which can contribute to the development of a sense of personal identity in the face of forces which often tend to alienate or estrange men from the organized centres of power. While most of us may agree with this article of faith—that elements of traditional culture should not be lost and means should be found to clarify their relevance—it is probably a task for the future to deal with these problems systematically and concretely.

7. We believe that the first and essential duty of the mass media in any given community is to return that community to itself. Communication should not be a one-way process. It must educate people about the present and the past, in recognition of a continuing process of social change; it should also serve as a means whereby these people can make their wishes known to the centres of power. It should allow the community by its participation at all levels to witness what it is doing, what it is feeling, what it is thinking. The second duty of mass media will be to extend this process of learning by making contact with other communities in order to create a constructive and continuing exchange between men wherever they may be. This, too, must not be a one-way process.

8. The freedom to know is a basic human right. We recognize that there must be some regulation of the media of communication in the interests of social order and stability (as there is in economic order, the control of aggression and other forms of disruption, transport regulations, and the maintenance of minimal standards of health). Nevertheless, the media of communication cannot be regarded exclusively as an arm or instrument of political or cultural control. Hence, we assert that: (a) means must be found to guarantee the full flow of information about contemporary events throughout the world; (b) means must be found to give the work of scientists, artists and other creative people the widest possible circulation, and the individual must have access to these; and (c) the individual's access, as receiver or participant, to these sources of

communication (such as newspapers, magazines, television receivers, radios) is a right that should not be violated by political authority.

9. To further implement the freedom to know as a basic human right, it is important to increase opportunities for more intimate interrelationships among the community of creative artists, the public of the arts and the public that is not at the moment involved in the creation and enjoyment of the arts. This would include more intensive dialogue and confrontation between the creative community and the recipient public.

10. Science and technology are continually changing man's world. This change is vast, comprehensive; and we must emphasize that men who are most deeply affected in every part of their life by these changes do not fully realize the significance of this process which involves them. Men must learn to accept that science, and the application of its results, will continue to form the background to all human culture. Education in science must become, therefore, the priority in the intellectual equipment of every individual. The perversion of science for political and commercial interests must be effectively checked if science is to be used in the service of man and for the enjoyment of all men.

11. The rights to culture include the possibility for each man to obtain the means of developing his personality, through his direct participation in the creation of human values, and of becoming, in this way, responsible for his situation, whether local or on a world scale.

CONCLUSION

We have only just begun. We have to hear from the people who have been rendered silent by their exclusion. And they have to hear from us. A continuing interaction must be established. Only then can we strengthen the concept of peace and understanding in the minds of men, and outlaw aggressiveness and war.

Appendixes

Appendixes

List of participants

Experts

Prof. Kiyotaka Aoyagi
Tokyo Women's Christian College
15-12, Imagawa 3-chome
Suginami-ku 167
Tokyo (Japan)

Prof. B. Boutros-Ghali
Cairo University
Giza
Cairo (United Arab Republic)

Mr. B. Breytenbach
15, rue Malebranche
75 Paris-5e (France)

Dr. Yehudi A. Cohen
Livinston College
Rutgers
The State University
New Brunswick, N.J. 08903
(United States of America)

Mr. Fernando Debesa
c/o Chilean Embassy
3 Hamilton Place
Park Lane
London, W.1 (United Kingdom)

Prof. Ernest A. Gellner
1908 Napa Avenue
Berkeley, Calif. 94707
(United States of America)

Mr. Francis Jeanson
Théâtre de Bourgogne
19, Avenue de la République
21 Beaune (France)

Mr. George Lamming
University of the West Indies
Mona (Jamaica)

Dr. Tomo Martelanc
Secretary for Education and Culture of
the Socialist Republic of Slovenia
Zupanciceva ul. 3-P: 644
Ljubljana (Yugoslavia)

Prof. Vladimir V. Mshvenieradze
Senior Research Officer
Institute of Philosophy of the U.S.S.R.
Academy of Sciences
Volhonka 14
Moscow (U.S.S.R.)

Prof. Alassane N'Daw
Professor of Philosophy at Dakar
University
Université de Dakar
Fann Parc
Dakar (Senegal)

Dr. Nicholas C. Otieno
University of East Africa
University College
P.O. Box 30197
Nairobi (Kenya)

Mr. Romesh Thapar
Director, India International Centre
40, Lodi Estate
New Delhi 3 (India)

Observers

Non-governmental organizations

International Social Science Council (ISSC)
Mr. K. Szczerba-Likiernik
Secretary-General
International Council for Philosophy
and Humanistic Studies (ICPHS)
Mr. J. d'Ormesson
Deputy Secretary-General
NGO Working Party on Human Rights
Dr. Claude Weil
Chairman
NGO Working Party on Culture
Mr. M. Gastaud
Chairman

Unesco Secretariat

*Department of Social Sciences,
Human Sciences and Culture*

Mr. Mahdi Elmandjra
Assistant Director-General for
Social Sciences, Human Sciences
and Culture

Mr. Harry Alpert
Director
Department of Social Sciences
Mr. Amadou Seydou
Director
Department of Culture
Miss Jeanne Hersch
Director
Division of Philosophy
Mrs. Marion Glean
Programme Specialist
Department of Social Sciences

Department of Mass Communication

Mr. William Farr
Director
Department of Mass Communication
Mr. Syed Waliullah
Programme Specialist
Department of Mass Communication

Agenda

1. Opening of the meeting

2. Adoption of the provisional agenda

3. General discussion of the broad concepts of cultural rights

4. The concept of cultural rights as human rights in 1948 and in 1968 in different socio-economic conditions (industrial and developing societies):
   (a) Rights of the individual
   (b) Community or group rights
   (c) 'Elitist' versus 'mass' conceptions

5. Factors influencing cultural rights as human rights:
   (a) Tradition
   (b) Education
   (c) Mass media
   (d) Cultural interaction
   (e) Socio-economic conditions
   (f) Social role of artists and writers

6. Measures being taken currently to implement these rights

7. The relationship of these rights to other provisions of the Universal Declaration of Human Rights.

Report of the meeting

The following report was adopted by the participants.

One may ask: 'What is this thing called culture and what is it for?' The answer is: culture does not serve any one purpose or set of purposes, but is, as it were, the medium through which all purposes are articulated and through which we live our lives. Normally, we take it for granted.

Culture is like prose—people who speak it do not normally classify it as such or even think about it in any kind of a way. Something, however, shocked Monsieur Jourdain into surprised realization that he had been speaking prose all his life, and something had similarly shocked the participants of the meeting into a heightened awareness of the problems of culture.

This is probably the best starting point: just what are those problems which make the otherwise almost unconscious culture into an object of concern? Much of the discussion was, in fact, about this background situation which makes culture problematic.

The factors most frequently cited were: underdevelopment, deprivation, oppression, political centralization, cultural neo-colonialism, misuse of mass media, imitativeness and revivalism. It should be noted that some of these are contradictory, and also that the manner in which they raise problems for culture are diverse and sometimes opposed. Oppression, deprivation and underdevelopment, as it were, bar access to any kind of culture; cultural neo-colonialism, unselective imitativeness or uncritical revivalism create cultures which are, in some way or other, false or misguided.

There was general agreement to the effect that, in the developing world, the improvement of economic and social conditions was the prime and absolute precondition of either the presence or the enjoyment of culture. There was much discussion, however, concerning whether a reaffirmation of local traditions was the condition or an obstacle for development. There was no disagreement about the supreme importance of education: in the developing world the right to culture is in substance the right to education. The group was also in agreement in feeling that culture was something that should be universally diffused and enjoyed, rather than restricted to an élite, and that mass participation in it must be one of the prime objectives. Rights to culture, like any others, involve duties—in this case the duty to ensure the implementation of these rights.

Many participants in the discussion felt that the problem of culture was just as acute in affluent societies as it is in developing ones, that the failures of communication and the cultural chasms were as grave and dangerous in this area as in any other. An alternative formulation was that in developed societies the individual was bombarded by the mass media with such a multiplicity of messages that the result cancelled out, or worse. By contrast, in developing countries the main problem is still the acquisition of adequate means of communication. Particularly important is the development and production of simple technological stereotypes and their provision, which would make mass media more accessible to the broad masses. Members of the group were concerned with the blocking of such developments by vested interests. They were, indeed, concerned with the general problem of power—who controls the cultural means of communication and for what end?

Their concern with this problem of power was complemented by a feeling of personal impotence and worry as to whether their ideas could be effectively implemented. They hoped that international institutions could be strengthened or established in order to assist such implementation. Suggestions were made for the increase of cultural interchange, for correcting the 'one-sided pipeline' of cultural flow between the rich and the developing countries, and for counteracting the distorting influences which diminish the range and effectiveness of mass media. The suggestions for increasing interchange included the establishment of a kind of international youth voluntary service. The theme of alienation was raised, affecting, as it does, culture in both kinds of contexts, and the need for culture to give a meaning to life.

The group was concerned with the existence of a cultural 'non-public', a large segment of the population which is culturally disinherited, and stressed the urgent need for finding a way of including it in full cultural citizenship.

The group was also concerned with the general issue of human subjection to the ill-understood consequences of technological control, of the importance of power. It noted the tendency to consider various developments as 'inevitable', on slender and inadequate evidence, and stressed the need to explore more thoroughly just what are the real options and the real inevitabilities of our collective situation.

One of the central issues which haunted most aspects of the discussion was: the escape from deprivation and underdevelopment requires modernization, industrialization and technological borrowing, but at the same time these very processes lead to the adulteration of culture, to cultural provincialism and to lack of cultural independence, which was equally deplored. This is, perhaps, the main problem which emerges from the discussion.

This problem could be summed up as the conflict between the right to culture and the rights of cultures. The first is the right of individuals to access to culture, of which they can be deprived by poverty or political oppression. The second is the right of cultures to survive in face of a radical transformation of the modern world. The first right requires modernization, the second has much to fear from it.

This, starkly presented, is the conflict. Theoretically, certain extreme solutions are available. One could, for instance, maintain an extreme cultural relativism, to the effect that all cultures are valuable and valid in their own terms and ought to be preserved, and that any interference or evaluation 'from the outside' is to be avoided. Alternatively, one could adopt the opposite extreme and say that certain situations are so intolerable that only a literally revolutionary break with the past and a cultural rebirth are acceptable. On the whole, these extreme solutions were not put forward. The main tendency was for the participants to seek some kind of middle way out between these extreme alternatives. A formulation which was frequently encountered was a stress on separating desirable from undesirable cultural borrowing, and desirable from undesirable preservation of tradition.

The conflict between the individual's right to culture and the rights of cultures is, of course

115

only part of their relationship. Man does not live by economic development alone, though it certainly looks as if he needs economic development to live at all; he also finds fulfilment in identification, activity, communication, pride. These all require a local culture through which he can identify and communicate. Many participants were concerned with the cultural 'bovaryism' by which a society loses confidence in itself and seeks fulfilment and criteria elsewhere.

The problem could also be formulated in a different kind of way. The rights of man which provide a basis for the discussion are not really neutral as between cultures. They presuppose certain values, notably liberty, human equality and democratic government (whilst bearing in mind that these values are not completely realized anywhere, and that their proclamation and their implementation are not necessarily identical). At the same time obviously not all cultures endorse these values, or endorse them to the same degree. Hence a brutal and insensitive and immediate implementation of these values would mean the endorsement of some cultures and the condemnation of others. Yet, this cannot be the intention of those who drew up the Universal Declaration of Human Rights, nor indeed is it the wish of the participants of the meeting, however much they may endorse that Declaration. This is a contradiction between a respect for man and a respect for cultures. One can be in favour of the defence of fragile cultures against cultural neo-colonialism, or in favour of utmost liberty in cultural sampling, a kind of universal free market in cultural styles, and one is tempted to be in favour of both. This contradiction is, of course, not a consequence of careless thinking: it follows directly and inevitably from the very nature of the situation.

This contradiction also illuminates a certain duality of meaning of the term 'culture' which pervades all discussions of it. Culture can be used in what is sometimes referred to as the élite sense, as something which is in short supply, particularly for the underprivileged sections of mankind, or it can be used in the anthropological sense, meaning roughly the distinctive style of life of a given community. The élite sense is relevant to the right of individuals to culture, whereas the anthropological sense is relevant to the right of cultures to survive.

The discussion went into many specific aspects of this general problem, such as: to what extent is political centralization either inevitable or culturally corrosive? What is the explanation of the paradox that precisely those cultural producers most anxious to reach the masses are in practice the least successful in doing so, while those most unconcerned with it are relatively more successful? Why does a Gresham's Law apply to cultural exchange? Can Unesco programmes for translating classics avoid giving the impression that achievement is mainly in the past? Are universities a good channel for transmitting culture? Are they necessarily conservative? How can cultural pluralism be combined with political unity—or, the centralization of modern life with fuller participation—and borrowing be achieved without domination or provincialization?

These issues were illustrated by numerous accounts of specific local situations, which it is impossible to summarize in this report.

Universal Declaration of Human Rights

Preamble

WHEREAS recognition of the inherent dignity and of the equal and inalienable rights of all members of the human family is the foundation of freedom, justice and peace in the world,

WHEREAS disregard and contempt for human rights have resulted in barbarous acts which have outraged the conscience of mankind, and the advent of a world in which human beings shall enjoy freedom of speech and belief and freedom from fear and want has been proclaimed as the highest aspiration of the common people,

WHEREAS it is essential, if man is not to be compelled to have recourse, as a last resort, to rebellion against tyranny and oppression, that human rights should be protected by the rule of law,

WHEREAS it is essential to promote the development of friendly relations between nations,

WHEREAS the peoples of the United Nations have in the Charter reaffirmed their faith in fundamental human rights, in the dignity and worth of the human person and in the equal rights of men and women and have determined to promote social progress and better standards of life in larger freedom,

WHEREAS Member States have pledged themselves to achieve, in co-operation with the United Nations, the promotion of universal respect for and observance of human rights and fundamental freedoms,

WHEREAS a common understanding of these rights and freedoms is of the greatest importance for the full realization of this pledge,

Now, therefore,

THE GENERAL ASSEMBLY PROCLAIMS

THIS UNIVERSAL DECLARATION OF HUMAN RIGHTS as a common standard of achievement for all peoples and all nations, to the end that every individual and every organ of society, keeping this Declaration constantly in mind, shall strive by teaching and education to promote respect for these rights and freedoms and by progressive measures, national and international, to secure their universal and effective recognition and observance, both among the peoples of Member States themselves and among the peoples of territories under their jurisdiction.

Article 1

All human beings are born free and equal in dignity and rights. They are endowed with reason and conscience and should act towards one another in a spirit of brotherhood.

Article 2

Everyone is entitled to all the rights and freedoms set forth in this Declaration, without distinction of any kind, such as race, colour, sex, language, religion, political or other opinion, national or social origin, property, birth or other status.

Furthermore, no distinction shall be made on the basis of the political, jurisdictional or international status of the country or territory to which a person belongs, whether it be independent, trust, non-self-governing or under any other limitation of sovereignty.

Article 3

Everyone has the right to life, liberty and security of person.

Article 4

No one shall be held in slavery or servitude; slavery and the slave trade shall be prohibited in all their forms.

Article 5

No one shall be subjected to torture or to cruel, inhuman or degrading treatment or punishment.

Article 6

Everyone has the right to recognition everywhere as a person before the law.

Article 7

All are equal before the law and are entitled without any discrimination to equal protection of the law. All are entitled to equal protection against any discrimination in violation of this Declaration and against any incitement to such discrimination.

Article 8

Everyone has the right to an effective remedy by the competent national tribunals for acts violating the fundamental rights granted him by the constitution or by law.

Article 9

No one shall be subjected to arbitrary arrest, detention or exile.

Article 10

Everyone is entitled in full equality to a fair and public hearing by an independent and impartial tribunal, in the determination of his rights and obligations and of any criminal charge against him.

Article 11

(1) Everyone charged with a penal offence has the right to be presumed innocent until proved guilty according to law in a public trial at which he has had all the guarantees necessary for his defence.

(2) No one shall be held guilty of any penal offence on account of any act or omission which did not constitute a penal offence, under national or international law, at the time when it was committed. Nor shall a heavier penalty be imposed than the one that was applicable at the time the penal offence was committed.

Article 12

No one shall be subjected to arbitrary interference with his privacy, family, home or correspondence. nor to attacks upon his honour and reputation. Everyone has the right to the protection of the law against such interference or attacks.

Article 13

(1) Everyone has the right to freedom of movement and residence within the borders of each State.

(2) Everyone has the right to leave any country, including his own, and to return to his country.

Article 14

(1) Everyone has the right to seek and to enjoy in other countries asylum from persecution.

(2) This right may not be invoked in the case of prosecutions genuinely arising from non-political crimes or from acts contrary to the purpose and principles of the United Nations.

Article 15

(1) Everyone has the right to a nationality.

(2) No one shall be arbitrarily deprived of his nationality nor denied the right to change his nationality.

Article 16

(1) Men and women of full age, without any limitation due to race, nationality or religion, have the right to marry and to found a family. They are entitled to equal rights as to marriage, during marriage and at its dissolution.

(2) Marriage shall be entered into only with the free and full consent of the intending spouses.

(3) The family is the natural and fundamental group unit of society and is entitled to protection by society and the State.

Article 17

(1) Everyone has the right to own property alone as well as in association with others.

(2) No one shall be arbitrarily deprived of his property.

Article 18

Everyone has the right to freedom of thought, conscience and religion; this right includes freedom to change his religion or belief, and freedom, either alone or in community with others and in public or private, to manifest his religion or belief in teaching, practice, worship and observance.

Article 19

Everyone has the right to freedom of opinion and expression; this right includes freedom to hold opinions without interference and to seek, receive and impart information and ideas through any media and regardless of frontiers.

Article 20

(1) Everyone has the right to freedom of peaceful assembly and association.

(2) No one may be compelled to belong to an association.

Article 21

(1) Everyone has the right to take part in the government of his country, directly or through freely chosen representatives.

(2) Everyone has the right of equal access to public service in his country.

(3) The will of the people shall be the basis of the authority of government; this will shall be expressed in periodic and genuine elections which shall be by universal and equal suffrage and shall be held by secret vote or by equivalent free voting procedures.

Article 22

Everyone, as a member of society, has the right to social security and is entitled to realization, through national effort and international co-operation and in accordance with the organization and resources of each State, of the economic, social and cultural rights indispensable for his dignity and the free development of his personality.

Article 23

(1) Everyone has the right to work, to free choice of employment, to just and favourable conditions of work and to protection against unemployment.

(2) Everyone, without any discrimination, has the right to equal pay for equal work.

(3) Everyone who works has the right to just and favourable remuneration ensuring for himself and his family an existence worthy of human dignity, and supplemented, if necessary, by other means of social protection.

(4) Everyone has the right to form and to join trade unions for the protection of his interests.

Article 24

Everyone has the right to rest and leisure, including reasonable limitation of working hours and periodic holidays with pay.

Article 25

(1) Everyone has the right to a standard of living adequate for the health and well-being of himself and of his family, including food, clothing, housing and medical care and necessary social services, and the right to security in the event of unemployment, sickness, disability, widowhood, old age or other lack of livelihood in circumstances beyond his control.

(2) Motherhood and childhood are entitled to special care and assistance. All children, whether born in or out of wedlock, shall enjoy the same social protection.

Article 26

(1) Everyone has the right to education. Education shall be free, at least in the elementary and fundamental stages. Elementary education shall be compulsory. Technical and professional education shall be made generally available and higher education shall be equally accessible to all on the basis of merit.

(2) Education shall be directed to the full development of the human personality and to the strengthening of respect for human rights and fundamental freedoms. It shall promote understanding, tolerance and friendship among all nations, racial or religious groups, and shall further the activities of the United Nations for the maintenance of peace.

(3) Parents have a prior right to choose the kind of education that shall be given to their children.

Article 27

(1) Everyone has the right freely to participate in the cultural life of the community, to enjoy the arts and to share in scientific advancement and its benefits.

(2) Everyone has the right to the protection of the moral and material interests resulting from any scientific, literary or artistic production of which he is the author.

Article 28

Everyone is entitled to a social and international order in which the rights and freedoms set forth in this Declaration can be fully realized.

Article 29

(1) Everyone has duties to the community in which alone the free and full development of his personality is possible.

(2) In the exercise of his rights and freedoms, everyone shall be subject only to such limitations as are determined by law solely for the purpose of securing due recognition and respect for the rights and freedoms of others and of meeting the just requirements of morality, public order and the general welfare in a democratic society.

(3) These rights and freedoms may in no case be exercised contrary to the purposes and principles of the United Nations.

Article 30

Nothing in this Declaration may be interpreted as implying for any State, group or person any right to engage in any activity or to perform any act aimed at the destruction of any of the rights and freedoms set forth herein.

Declaration of the Principles of International Cultural Co-operation

THE GENERAL CONFERENCE of the United Nations Educational, Scientific and Cultural Organization, met in Paris for its fourteenth session, this fourth day of November 1966, being the twentieth anniversary of the foundation of the Organization,

RECALLING that the Constitution of the Organization declares that 'since wars begin in the minds of men, it is in the minds of men that the defences of peace must be constructed' and that the peace must be founded, if it is not to fail, upon the intellectual and moral solidarity of mankind,

RECALLING that the Constitution also states that the wide diffusion of culture and the education of humanity for justice and liberty and peace are indispensable to the dignity of man and constitute a sacred duty which all the nations must fulfil in a spirit of mutual assistance and concern,

CONSIDERING that the Organization's Member States, believing in the pursuit of truth and the free exchange of ideas and knowledge, have agreed and determined to develop and to increase the means of communication between their peoples,

CONSIDERING that, despite the technical advances which facilitate the development and dissemination of knowledge and ideas, ignorance of the way of life and customs of peoples still presents an obstacle to friendship among the nations, to peaceful co-operation and to the progress of mankind,

TAKING ACCOUNT of the Universal Declaration of Human Rights, the Declaration of the Rights of the Child, the Declaration on the Granting of Independence to Colonial Countries and Peoples, the United Nations Declaration on the Elimination of all Forms of Racial Discrimination, the Declaration on the Promotion among Youth of the Ideals of Peace, Mutual Respect and Understanding between Peoples, and the Declaration on the Inadmissibility of Intervention in the Domestic Affairs of States and the Protection of their Independence and Sovereignty, proclaimed successively by the General Assembly of the United Nations,

CONVINCED by the experience of the Organization's first twenty years that, if international cultural co-operation is to be strengthened, its principles require to be affirmed,

PROCLAIMS this Declaration of the principles of international cultural co-operation, to the end that governments, authorities, organizations, associations and institutions responsible for cultural activities may constantly be guided by these principles; and for the purpose, as set out in the Constitution of the Organization, of advancing, through the educational, scientific and cultural relations of the peoples of the world, the objectives of peace and welfare that are defined in the Charter of the United Nations:

Article I

1. Each culture has a dignity and value which must be respected and preserved.
2. Every people has the right and the duty to develop its culture.
3. In their rich variety and diversity, and in the reciprocal influences they exert on one another, all cultures form part of the common heritage belonging to all mankind.

Article II

Nations shall endeavour to develop the various branches of culture side by side and, as far as possible, simultaneously, so as to establish a harmonious balance between technical progress and the intellectual and moral advancement of mankind.

Article III

International cultural co-operation shall cover all aspects of intellectual and creative activities relating to education, science and culture.

Article IV

The aims of international cultural co-operation in its various forms, bilateral or multilateral, regional or universal, shall be:
1. To spread knowledge, to stimulate talent and to enrich cultures;
2. To develop peaceful relations and friendship among the peoples and bring about a better understanding of each other's way of life;
3. To contribute to the application of the principles set out in the United Nations Declarations that are recalled in the Preamble to this Declaration;
4. To enable everyone to have access to knowledge, to enjoy the arts and literature of all peoples, to share in advances made in science in all parts of the world and in the resulting benefits, and to contribute to the enrichment of cultural life;
5. To raise the level of the spiritual and material life of man in all parts of the world.

Article V

Cultural co-operation is a right and a duty for all peoples and all nations, which should share with one another their knowledge and skills.

Article VI

International co-operation, while promoting the enrichment of all cultures through its beneficent action, shall respect the distinctive character of each.

Article VII

1. Broad dissemination of ideas and knowledge, based on the the freest exchange and discussion, is essential to creative activity, the pursuit of truth and the development of the personality.

2. In cultural co-operation, stress shall be laid on ideas and values conducive to the creation of a climate of friendship and peace. Any mark of hostility in attitudes and in expression of opinion shall be avoided. Every effort shall be made, in presenting and disseminating information, to ensure its authenticity.

Article VIII

Cultural co-operation shall be carried on for the mutual benefit of all the nations practising it. Exchange to which it gives rise shall be arranged in a spirit of broad reciprocity.

Article IX

Cultural co-operation shall contribute to the establishment of stable, long-term relations between peoples, which should be subjected as little as possible to the strains which may arise in international life.

Article X

Cultural co-operation shall be specially concerned with the moral and intellectual education of young people in a spirit of friendship, international understanding and peace and shall foster awareness among States of the need to stimulate talent and promote the training of the rising generations in the most varied sectors.

Article XI

1. In their cultural relations, States shall bear in mind the principles of the United Nations. In seeking to achieve international co-operation, they shall respect the sovereign equality of States and shall refrain from intervention in matters which are essentially within the domestic jurisdiction of any State.

2. The principles of this Declaration shall be applied with due regard for human rights and fundamental freedoms.